GANGS AND GIRLS

BY MICHEL DORAIS

English (published by McGill-Queen's University Press, Montreal and Kingston)

Don't Tell: The Sexual Abuse of Boys, 2002
Dead Boys Can't Dance: Sexual Orientation, Masculinity, and Suicide (with Simon Lajeunesse), 2004
Rent Boys: The World of Male Sex Workers, 2005

French (published by VLB Éditeur, Montreal)

Les enfants de la prostitution (with Denis Ménard), 1987
L'Homme désemparé, 1988
Les lendemains de la révolution sexuelle, 1990
Tous les hommes le font, 1991
La peur de l'autre en soi (edited with Daniel Welzer-Lang and Pierre Dutey), 1994
La mémoire du désir, 1995
Ça arrive aussi aux garçons, 1997
Éloge de la diversité sexuelle, 1999
Mort ou fif (with Simon Louis Lajeunesse), 2001
Travailleurs du sexe, 2003

Portuguese (published by Ediçoes Loyola, Sao Paulo)

O homem desamparado, 1994
O erotismo masculino, 1994

Gangs and Girls

Understanding Juvenile Prostitution

MICHEL DORAIS AND PATRICE CORRIVEAU

TRANSLATED BY
PETER FELDSTEIN

McGill-Queen's University Press
Montreal & Kingston · London · Ithaca

ISBN 978-0-7735-3441-4 (cloth)
ISBN 978-0-7735-3442-1 (paper)

Legal deposit first quarter 2009
Bibliothèque nationale du Québec

Printed in Canada on acid-free paper that is 100% ancient forest free (100% post-consumer recycled), processed chlorine free.

Originally published as *Jeunes filles sous influence* by VLB in 2006.

Translation of this book was made possible by a grant from the Translation Program of the Canada Council for the Arts.

McGill-Queen's University Press acknowledges the support of the Canada Council for the Arts for our publishing program. We also acknowledge the financial support of the Government of Canada through the Book Publishing Industry Development Program (BPIDP) for our publishing activities.

Library and Archives Canada Cataloguing in Publication

Dorais, Michel, 1954–
Gangs and girls: understanding juvenile prostitution / Michel Dorais and Patrice Corriveau; translated by Peter Feldstein.

Translation of: Jeunes filles sous influence.
Includes bibliographical references and index.
ISBN 978-0-7735-3441-4 (bnd)
ISBN 978-0-7735-3442-1 (pbk)

1. Teenage prostitution – Canada. 2. Child prostitution – Canada. 3. Prostitutes – Canada – Social conditions. 4. Gangs – Canada. I. Corriveau, Patrice, 1974– II. Feldstein, Peter, 1962– III. Title.
HQ149.Q8.D67213 2008 306.74′50971 C2008-903885-1

This book was typeset by Interscript Inc. in 11/15 Sabon.

Contents

Acknowledgments

We would like to thank Isabelle Thibodeau, Denis-Philippe Paradis, Travis Earl, and Myriam Dion for their valuable contributions to this research project. Special thanks also to the Groupe de travail régional sur la prostitution juvenile (Working Group on Juvenile Prostitution of Quebec City), organized by Centre Jeunesse de Québec (Quebec Youth Centre), whose participants generously helped us to enhance and validate the analysis. Particularly helpful among them was Nathalie Thériault; her expertise and perspicacity were most appreciated. Laurent Aubut did much to facilitate and encourage our work with the police. Finally, the first French edition of this work greatly benefited from the sage advice of Robert Laliberté, literary director at VLB Éditeur.

Preface

The phone started ringing at five A.M. The original French edition of this book had just come out, and already it seemed that everyone wanted to know what we knew about the lives of prostituted girls. By day's end one of the authors had given sixteen interviews to radio, television, and print media. A month later the tally stood at about one hundred. Thousand of copies of the book had been sold, and it was in its fourth printing. For a short period *Jeunes filles sous influence* was only kept out of the top spot on Quebec's bestseller lists by none other than the latest Harry Potter. Needless to say, as university researchers we weren't expecting such an overwhelming reaction, nor were our publishers. This book obviously answered a broadly felt need. The message we kept receiving from specialized practitioners such as social workers and police and from the general public was: You haven't just told us that teenage prostitution exists – you've shown us how it works. Since then we have been asked to speak before numerous specialist and generalist audiences.

Most of what goes on in a multi-year research project is fairly low profile, and this one was no exception. Certainly we assumed that our work would be well received. Given how little the phenomenon of juvenile prostitution has been documented in any language, we felt it should be possible to further society's understanding of prostitution with the ultimate goal of improving prevention efforts. But the unprecedented media visibility had an unexpected effect. Just a few days after the book was published, we began to receive e-mails and phone calls from social workers, police officers, parents, former victims, and even an ex-pimp, all of them encouraging us to pursue our study and offering new information. We thank these people for their contributions to an English version that has been revised and augmented to such an extent that it represents a new work. In particular, we have made an effort to expand the scope of our remarks beyond the Quebec and Canadian contexts. We also present here several new ideas about prevention, in response to requests and suggestions from practitioners whom we met at public events and conferences following the publication of the French version. In short, we have completed the work "in the heat of the action," giving consideration to new needs and new information as they arose. The result is a book that goes far beyond the scope of the small research grants with which it originated.

We look forward to seeing this book reach a new audience eager to understand a long-standing phenomenon whose seriousness is coming to be recognized.

Many girls caught up in prostitution are still waiting for help. Many others who have not yet met that fate need to know what lies in store for them, the better to turn their backs on street gangs. And there is one additional group that needs to be made the target of much more in the way of awareness-raising and prevention: the boys and men who lure teenage girls into prostitution.

FOREWORD

Researching Gang-Organized Juvenile Prostitution: Contributions and Challenges

The involvement of teenaged girls in gang-related prostitution is a continuous concern in many communities in Canada and abroad. Media headlines and government crime reports tell of predominantly middle-class female adolescents between the ages of twelve and eighteen being recruited into prostitution by male peers who are themselves often specifically targeted by organized crime. These male youth, vulnerable due to economic and other forms of marginalization, are typically promised gang membership in exchange for luring young women into the sex industry.

Gangs and Girls: Understanding Juvenile Prostitution by Michel Dorais and Patrice Corriveau, originally published in French in 2006 under the title *Jeunes filles sous influence: Prostitution juvénile et gangs de rue*, offers anglophone readers a rare account of the phenomenon of gang-controlled teen prostitution. This edition has been updated with additional information as well as prevention strategies that help readers think about the links among research, policy, and practice concerning gang-related juvenile prostitution. The book also brings to the foreground the difficulties of conducting research on this much debated but little understood social problem.

Dorais and Corriveau set as their central task to "understand how gang-controlled juvenile prostitution works, not to point the finger at its participants." Given this aim, *Gangs and Girls* is largely based on accounts offered to the researchers by social workers, community outreach staff, and police officers – those working to help teenaged girls trapped in gang-related prostitution principally in Quebec City and Montreal and surroundings areas to return to their families or otherwise set out on a new pathway to adulthood. The book also includes comments from a small number of girls who have been able to escape gang control, several parents whose daughters have been involved in gang-related prostitution, and one young man also with prior involvement. These accounts help the authors to move the literature on street gangs and juvenile prostitution beyond a traditional "delinquent" perspective and instead to expose the numerous ways that the young women and men involved in these gangs are themselves influenced by, and sometimes victims of, larger forces. The book sheds light on these vulnerable youth and the pathways they follow into and (for the most part) eventually out of street gangs.

According to Dorais and Corriveau, young women who become involved in gang-related prostitution share a desperate desire to be "liked, respected and acknowledged." While there is no "typical profile," the girls fall into one of four overlapping categories: *sex slaves*, forced into the trade against their will and often becoming drug addicted, *submissives*, emotionally dependent on boyfriends who end up pimping them, *independents*, involved for the money with the hope of a glamorous life, and *daredevils*, in for the thrill or adventure. According to the authors' data sources, numerous girls end up as either sex slaves or as submissives in danger of slipping into the slave group. The authors describe the highly controlled, repressive nature of juvenile prostitution by street gangs: the girls end up for the most part confined against their wills, belittled, sexually exploited, and pushed around by male gang members, including those who pimp them. The girls are routinely rough-handled and treated in a demeaning manner by most of the clients or "johns" they are forced to serve. In short, Dorais and Corriveau report, while some girls manage for a while to operate as independents or daredevils and may even aspire to become full-fledged members of street gangs, few are able to follow these alternative paths because of the strong macho culture of the street gangs and the traditional scripts that assign very narrow roles to both genders. So while some girls may resist the dominant sexual codes of the gang that put them in second place to male counterparts, in the end they struggle to protect their "sexual reputations," to avoid being seen as "easy" or a "whore."

Apart from its insights into the situation of the girls involved gang-related prostitution, *Gangs and Girls* makes a major contribution by going beyond a delinquency perspective on the boys who become gang members. We learn that these young males are by and large from economically and socially disadvantaged neighbourhoods. Many belong to visible minority communities or have recently immigrated; some are of Aboriginal background. Most have experienced discrimination and understand what it is like to be socially excluded from the resources enjoyed by more privileged males. It thus makes strategic sense that they become attached to street gangs, not unlike marginalized youth in earlier generations growing up in inner-city slums marked by ethnic division and class polarization.

Dorais and Corriveau describe street gangs as comprising three concentric circles. Located in the inner core are the leaders who give strategic direction and control much of the gang's earnings. The next circle is comprised of those members who display strong allegiance to the gang and frequently take part in gang activities but not on a full-time basis. In the outer circle of the gang are half or more of the members, some not yet teens, who exhibit the weakest affiliation to the gang and have to prove their loyalty before becoming accepted as full-fledged members. Entry rites include undergoing "punching initiations" (taking pain like a man and being beaten up without flinching) and doing battle with boys from rival gangs (inflicting pain on the enemy as demonstrated proof of gang loyalty and complicity). In this manner, "the marginalized, fearful boy becomes the person who incites fear, completing a vicious cycle in which anyone who does not wish to be hunted becomes a hunter." The final test for the young male gang aspirant is his ability to become a recruiter or pimp, which according to the authors has become one of the most lucrative street gang strategies in the study region. Recruitment involves attracting and seducing vulnerable girls through practices such as "love bombing" (showering them with goodies and feigned affections), ensuring their allegiance, and then displaying contempt for them through such rituals as the "gang-bang." Gang-bangs start out as "sex-ins" whereby the young recruiter entraps his girlfriend is a situation where she is forced to have sex with other gang members. The aim is to sexually desensitize both girlfriend and boyfriend, preparing them for their roles in the gang's juvenile prostitution activities. The young males soon become conditioned into pimping other prospective girlfriends, offering them up to clients willing to pay handsome sums for sex with these underage girls, most of whom see little of their earnings.

Dorais and Corriveau conclude their book with a list of recommendations for helping these girls turn their lives around. They argue that because some made a conscious choice to get involved in street-gang prostitution in the first place, suggestions to help them have to also be strategic and compelling, based on reasoning and realistic options rather than condemnation and duress. The authors also advocate practical interventions to help young males involved in street gangs find meaning and resources to reorganize their lives along legitimate lines. These involve alternative educational and employment options as well as opportunities to develop positive relationships with girls and women.

To illuminate the coercive activities that in different ways entrap vulnerable female and male youth in gang-related prostitution, Dorais and Corriveau rely largely on the reports from those who work with street- and prostitution-involved young people rather than from the youth themselves. This information is helpful in telling us how professionals conceive of, and experience, the problem of gang-related juvenile prostitution, yet we should not immediately assume that the young people themselves share the same viewpoints about their own situation.

The victimization-based perspective that in part shapes the authors' analysis can be traced in Canada back to the release of the *Badgley Report*.[1] Named after Robin Badgley, the sociologist who chaired the commission responsible for the report, it marked the beginning of a shift from viewing youth as responsible for their plight ("juvenile delinquents") to a more humanistic and caring perspective that saw them as victims of societal forces and others' wrongdoings: hence the change in terminology to "exploited," "abandoned," or "discarded" youth or related terms. This perspective is highly gendered, mainly concerned with how female youth, without the protection of their families, are open targets for manipulation and exploitation of others. On the street, these vulnerable girls are seen as falling prey to male recruiters who make them drug dependent and force them into trading sex for money or in-kind goods.[2] According to Bagley and Young (1987), "the girl who finally tries prostitution is one who is already degraded and demoralized, in a state of psychological bondage, with grossly diminished self confidence." Advocates of the victimization perspective argue that the individuals exploiting these vulnerable female youth also take advantage of their feelings of disconnectedness and low self-esteem and isolation and, in some cases, their substance addictions and health and school related problems.

Dorais and Corriveau's book is organized around this humanistic, gendered discourse. The authors argue that "the street, as a public space, is seen as an ideal setting in which to affirm one's manhood, contrary to the home or private space, which remains the domain of female expression, at least as generally conceived of in our culture." Here as in many other parts of the book it is assumed that, with a few exceptions, youth involved in street gangs are eventually forced to see themselves as gendered opposites: females as weak, submissive, sexually dependent, hungry for male attention and approval, males as strong, dominant, sexually aggressive, sexual promiscuous. Thus, while both girls and boys are influenced by larger social forces, it is the girls who get the worse end of the stick because it is they who almost always get sexually (as well as physically) exploited. Juvenile prostitution is just the next step along their victimization pathway.

Nevertheless, it is important for all researchers to strive to capture the true diversity of street-involved youth, if only to avoid tarring all of them with the same brush – helpless victims. The "victim" label not only stigmatizes them but also deprives them of a sense of self. Young people's agency in organizing their lives, on the street or elsewhere, has important implications for the implementation and delivery of effective programs and interventions.

Recently, social and health science researchers have begun to round out academic knowledge of adult sex workers and the variations among members of that group. Many of these scholars have undertaken studies with community partners in order to address shortcomings in the literature. These studies move beyond a limited inquiry of street-based female workers to include males, transsexual and transgender people, and individuals working in non-street sectors of the industry where it is estimated 80–85 per cent of the population is located.[3] Preliminary findings show that several forces contribute to important differences within the population; these include gender, membership in other vulnerable populations including Aboriginals and visible minority groups, the sociolegal environments in which the activities take place, the degree of discrimination they experience and internalize, the extent to which people in their intimate networks support their work, and – pertinent to Dorais and Corriveau's book – their age of entry, intensity, and length of involvement in the industry.

In summary, *Gangs and Girls* makes an important contribution to the growing academic scholarship on juvenile prostitution. The authors offer a well-written, concise, and exciting professional account of the plight of vulnerable girls who become involved in street gangs and often find themselves selling sex against their will, as well as of the boys who learn to become sexual exploiters. In suggesting ways of helping vulnerable youth, the book will be of interest not only to academics but also to social workers, police, and other service professionals as well as teachers, parents and other members of the larger community. No doubt the book will also stimulate further research in order to fill in knowledge gaps to inform interventions tailored the specific needs and concerns of the youth themselves.

Cecilia Benoit

NOTES

1 R. Badgley, *Sexual Offences against Children: Report of the Committee on Sexual Offences against Children and Youths* (Ottawa: Canadian Government Publishing, 1984).
2 C. Bagley and L. Young, "Juvenile Prostitution and Child Sexual Abuse: A Controlled Study," *Canadian Journal of Community Mental Health* 6 (1987): 5–25.
3 See *Canadian Review of Sociology and Anthropology* 43, no. 3 (2006), special issue, *Critical Perspectives on Sex Industry Work in Canada*.

GANGS AND GIRLS

Introduction

For a semblance of love, for money quickly earned and just as quickly spent, for a thrill or an adventure, or in some cases for no other reason than that they are coerced into it, many teenage girls today find themselves in the world of prostitution. They are the bread and butter of street gangs, for prostituting girls is a lucrative business and there is no shortage of new recruits. Yet the subject remains notably absent from academic gang studies. Do scholars consider it taboo, perhaps? The media for their part miss no opportunity to cover juvenile prostitution stories.

In recent years the police have cracked down on gang-related juvenile prostitution rings,[1] and this illicit business suddenly became highly visible in the media. The general public was hungry for information, asking questions such as: Why do street gangs exist and why are they on the rise? Why do they prostitute girls? Why do so many girls fall prey to them? What is it about gang members that these girls are attracted to? Why do some girls appear to be "consenting victims"? Do prostituted girls come from typical backgrounds or profiles? What are the effects of this work on their physical, mental, and emotional health? Why has prostitution become such a major source of revenuc for street gangs? Why and how do street gangs control other criminal activities revolving around prostitution? What are the relationships between street gangs and organized crime? Why do so many clients ("johns") want to have sex with minors? And why is it so difficult to dismantle these rings and identify their clients?

These questions guided our initial literature review (in French and English), our subsequent interviews with numerous practitioners in this field (social workers, educators, police officers, street workers, and community organizations), and our interviews with young women who have been prostituted. Our goal was to understand the dynamics of gang-controlled prostitution. How does it work, and why? What are the motivations of the interested parties – the pimps, the prostitutes, and the clients, not to mention the criminal organizations with which the street gangs must do business in order to capture a share of the lucrative sex market?

We must clarify from the outset that this study does not deal with street gangs as such. Many excellent works on that subject already exist. Our specific purpose has been to study the operation of juvenile prostitution where it is initiated or controlled by gangs. Since all signs are that this worrisome trend is on the rise, there is no doubt as to the importance of such an exploratory study.

As we gathered the materials necessary for our research, documentation, and interviews, a good deal of our work consisted of rethinking the phenomenon of underage prostitution and finding more suitable concepts with which to analyze it. Two theoretical tools – strategic analysis and gender analysis – seemed particularly appropriate, and we have made them central components of our analysis in this book. Strategic analysis strives to explain the motivations of persons or groups when they act in certain ways. The gangs, girls, and clients involved in gang-controlled juvenile prostitution comprise three different cultures or rationalities that have quite different sets of motivations for their actions. In fact, they can be said to inhabit parallel worlds that only intersect in the act of prostitution itself. Knowing these motivations can be a useful tool in prevention efforts.

As for gender analysis, it gives central explanatory power to the sex and gender of the participants in a given social interaction – in this case, prostituted teenagers and pimps. It seeks to understand how, why, and to what extent differences in status or roles can be related to the variable of gender. In a nutshell, and to make an obvious point, we are interested in why it is always groups of young men who prostitute young women and never the reverse.

Readers who open this book in the hope of finding scabrous details or information that could serve to identify individuals or groups should close it and look elsewhere. It was an ironclad rule in our research to throw out any information that might be used to trace a victim, a pimp, a client, or even a particular gang. We are social science researchers, not police investigators or journalists. Our goal here is to understand how gang-controlled juvenile prostitution works, not to point the finger at its participants. A final note: we wish to stress that our conclusions are ours alone. They do not necessarily reflect the opinions of persons or organizations we consulted or who gave us assistance.

1

What Is a Street Gang and How Is It Organized?

Although our study is not about street gangs as such, a brief description of the phenomenon is necessary as background material. We have relied, where possible, on Quebec and Canadian research, of which relatively little has been produced on the subject. Most of the available documentation comes from the United States. We have drawn on this literature, since the situation in Canada is influenced by what is going on in the United States.[2]

As Martin Scorsese's film *Gangs of New York* suggests, street gangs have roamed the large cities of North America since the nineteenth century, if not earlier (Asbury 1928; Hagedorn 1998; Vigil, 2002). The title of a 1927 study, *The Gang: A Study of 1,313 Gangs in Chicago* (Thrasher 1927), eloquently attests to how far things had gone by that time. Many of these gangs, comprising 25,000 youths in all – some as young as age six – would not be thought of as gangs today, since they were not highly criminalized or did not commit violent crimes.

The two large gang families that became the Bloods and the Crips in the 1970s were in fact the heirs to clubs formed in Los Angeles in the 1940s by young blacks as a defensive reaction against white violence. The racist Ku Klux Klan, moribund for decades, had resurfaced among the city's whites in response to a burgeoning black population. Gangs of young white men were trying to keep blacks out of "white" neighbourhoods, while blacks were rightly refusing to be ghettoized.[3] Thus, in their earliest incarnation, gangs were defensive rather than offensive entities.

The early 1970s saw the rise (in Los Angeles) of the modern, aggressive form of the street gang, which soon proliferated throughout the United States. Today's gangs can trace their heritage to that time. They consist of groups of adolescents and young adults identifiable at a glance by their chosen colours (blue or red), logos, graffiti, tattoos, ethnic and territorial allegiance and, most critically, by their criminal activities. While self-defence (from other gangs) is still a motivation, their prime goal is to make money through illicit activities and to inspire "respect," by intimidation if necessary. Many of their members feel unjustly marginalized, discriminated against, or excluded and are willing to consider various ways of taking justice into their own hands. Earning a living from illegal business is one of them.

The appearance of street gangs in Quebec and Canada dates from the 1980s, when these groups started to become larger, more visible, and more disruptive to authorities and residents. The young people of that time have grown up, and some gang members are now in their forties or fifties. As adolescents or young adults, they were introduced to a "good life" free of drudgery and revolving around instant gratification. They continue to live that life, paying for it out of the wages of crime. Some of them have become experienced criminals, rivalling the mafia for business acumen and propensity to violence (Thornberry et al. 2003). The criminologist Maurice Cusson (2005) notes that in most places where gangs operate, their members are the main perpetrators of violent crime.

Apart from their more traditional activities, gangs have taken control of bars and restaurants in Toronto, Montreal, and other large cities. Their threatening presence is often felt in public places such as metro stations. More recently, gangs have spread out to conquer medium-sized cities and suburbs where drugs and prostitution markets, as well as robbery and fraud, offer them attractive opportunities for growth. Wherever there is money to be made and power to be seized, a gang will be there to expand its "territory."[4]

The majority of experts agree that the number of gangs has not increased. However, their size has grown significantly from the 1970s to the present. As well, gangs are attracting youths at a progressively earlier age. It is not uncommon today for children of ten, eleven, or twelve to join. To prove their mettle, these young members may take part in "taxing" of other children at school. According to practitioners whom we interviewed, boys are frequently introduced to gang life by an older brother, stepfather, or other trusted person. By age six or seven, many of them already know the "colour" of the gang they will join in the near future. They begin by mimicking their role models and gradually develop an allegiance to gang culture.

According to the Quebec police authorities, the number of street gang members in the province has followed the North American pattern, at least tripling in fifteen years. Astwood Strategy Corporation (2002) found that 434 gangs comprising more than seven thousand members are operating in Canada and that at least seven of ten provinces are grappling with gang problems. Similarly, Criminal Intelligence Service Canada (CISC) has estimated the number of Canadian street gangs and members at three hundred and eleven thousand, respectively (CISC 2006), including about twenty gangs in British Columbia, thirty in Alberta, twenty-one in Saskatchewan, twenty-five in Manitoba, fifty in Quebec, 175 in Ontario, and about fifteen in the Atlantic provinces. Toronto alone accounts for some eighty active gangs. For the United States, the National Youth Gang Center (2006) has estimated the number of street gangs and members at 21,600 and 731,500, respectively, in 2002. More than 70 per cent of American cities are today inhabited by street gangs, as are many suburbs (Starbuck, Howell, and Lindquist 2001; Stinchcomb 2002).

However, these estimates require qualification. It is practically impossible to accurately assess an "underground" social phenomenon that is constantly shifting in space and time (Hagedorn 1998; Souillière 1998). Furthermore, it is difficult to assess a member's level of involvement when the definition of a street gang is itself controversial. Should a hanger-on who wears the gang's colours be thought of and treated the same way as a criminalized core member? Another problem: what determines when a person enters or leaves a gang? Hébert, Hamel, and Savoie (1997) found that the duration of preteen and teenage gang affiliation was often less than one year. Covey, Menard, and Franzese (1992), Spergel (1995), and Howell (2000) concur that gang participation is often a transitory experience. Since the membership and composition of gangs is constantly shifting, there is no way to provide an accurate account of their numbers. What no one disputes is that the phenomenon is on the rise and that recent crackdowns have not improved the situation (Spergel 1995; Howell 2000; Delaney 2006). Street gangs are increasingly visible to the media and the police, not least because of their involvement in juvenile prostitution.

There is still no consensus as to the definition of a street gang, and interpretations of the phenomenon are still being refined.[5] While the police focus on the criminal and violent aspects of gangs, social workers tend to interpret them as groupings of troubled youths. The Montreal police department, for example, defines a street gang as a group of adolescents or young adults who regularly use force and intimidation in the context of committing violent crimes.[6] Six criteria are used to confirm the existence of a street gang:

1. a structure or degree of organization;
2. an identifiable leadership;
3. a specific territory;
4. regular association with and among several juvenile delinquents;
5. specific goals pursued by the group; and
6. participation in illegal activities.

More schematically, Fournier, Cousineau, and Hamel (2004) define gangs as "groups of adolescents and/or young adults with a degree of organization who commit crimes, notably violent crimes." What is the difference between street gangs and other youth or delinquent associations? Hamel et al. (1998) identify six types of gangs according to their levels on a continuum of violence, criminality, and organization:

1. pseudo-gangs, composed of teenagers who identify with gangs and attempt to imitate their behaviour;
2. territorial gangs, composed of teenagers concerned mainly with issues of prestige and protection of an urban territory;
3. delinquent groups, composed of teenagers who commit delinquent and violent acts but to a lesser degree than street gangs;
4. violent ideological gangs, such as certain skinhead groups;
5. street gangs proper, composed of teenagers and young adults who are involved in illegal, criminal, and violent activities;

6 criminal organizations, involving youths and adults organized into structured, hierarchical, relatively stable groups engaged in criminal activity for rapid economic gain.

Figure 1 (from Guay, 2007) illustrates this continuum.

This typology has the advantage of situating street gangs among other groupings with which they might be confused. Several observers note that violence and crime do not make up the daily routine of street gangs, who spend much of their time in loitering and idleness. Only a small percentage of gang members ultimately become

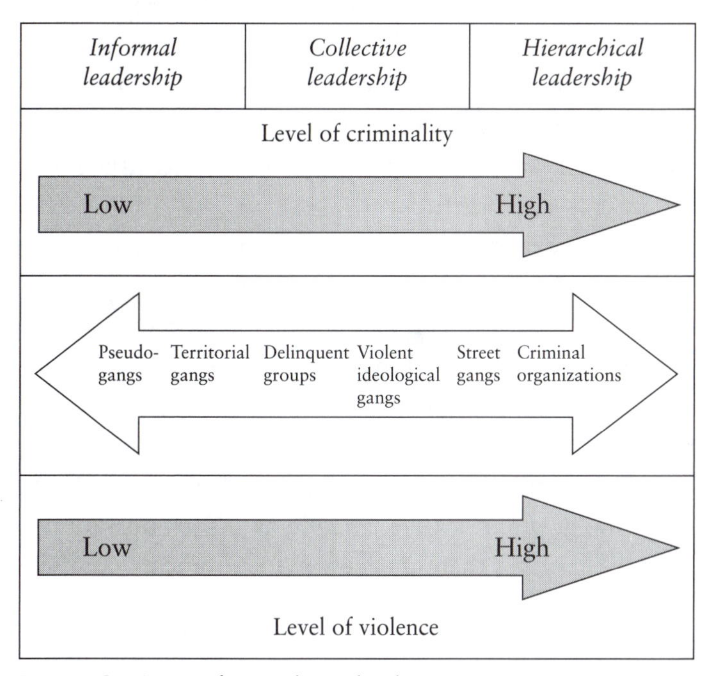

Figure 1 Continuum of criminality and violence

regular or repeat criminals. However, Perreault (2005) summarizes the position of a majority of the practitioners we interviewed: "Belonging to a gang means accepting and identifying with a certain level of violence, even though the gang member may not at first be fully aware of its grave implications."

A common model used to describe street gang organization consists of three concentric circles (Vigil 1990; Spergel 1995; Tichit 2003; figure 2). In the centre are the leaders, accounting for 10 to 15 per cent of the members. They decide how the gang will operate and what it will do, and generally have a pseudonym reflecting their position of dominance ("King," "Chief," etc.). They are generally the ones with the greatest propensity for violence and crime (most importantly for our purposes here, prostitution) and the ones who profit most from it. The more money there is to be made, the more the leaders exert their control.

In the next circle are found approximately 30 to 40 per cent of the members, who identify strongly with the gang but do not devote all of their time to it and have little or no control over it. Generally less criminalized, they may engage in criminal pursuits at the behest of their leaders. Since their ties with the hard core are largely circumstantial, they may interact with more than one group at a time, as long as the groups are not rivals. This gives them the leeway to adjudicate conflicts or to act as intermediaries for weapon and drug purchases in which several gangs are involved.

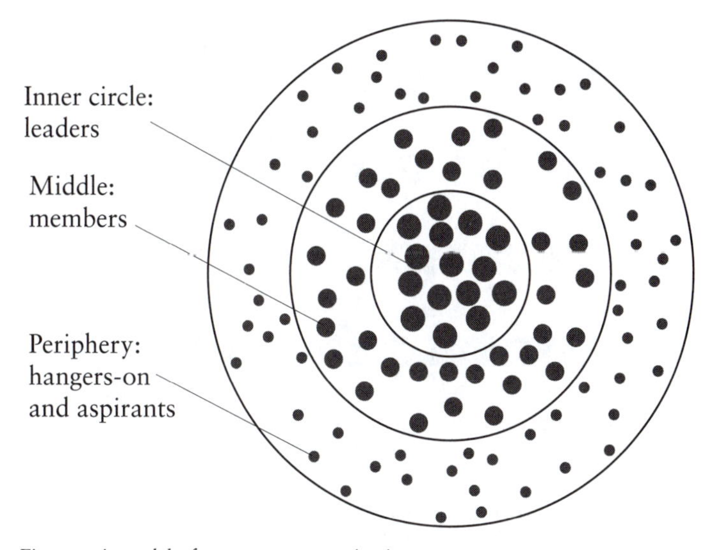

Figure 2 A model of street gang organization

On the periphery are the remaining 45 to 60 per cent of "hangers-on" who exhibit the weakest affiliation. This group also includes some preteen aspirants. A key aspect of the attraction of young teens to gangs, one that is often underestimated in studies on the subject, yet confirmed by all available data, is the perceived peer group status it gives them; proudly displaying the gang's colours, they inspire respect, fear, and envy in the kids around them. They have "succeeded." Still, this group's identification with the gang is less total and their participation more irregular than for inner-circle members.

While the typology just presented is of some use in categorizing street gang members, the reality is much more complex than it suggests. A multidimensional

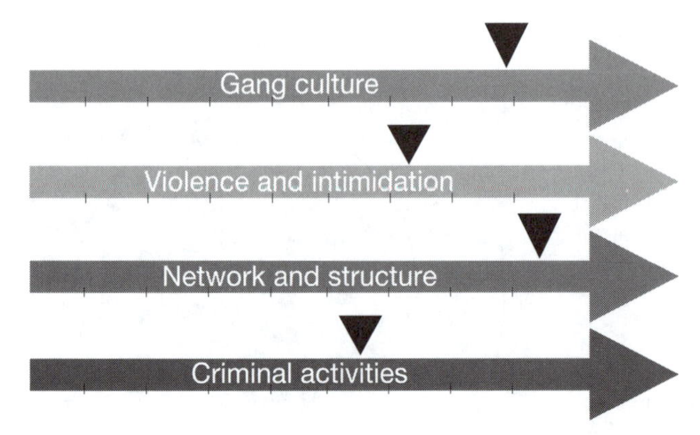

Figure 3 A multi-dimensional model of gang membership

model can better and more dynamically account for the many characteristics that serve as indicators of the strength of a boy's allegiance to a gang over time, and any changes in gang internal structure that this may imply. The portrait that emerges is more sensitive to the individual's needs and a better guide to intervention. Guay (2007) presents a model based on four variables: 1) display of gang culture, as determined by clothing type and colour, tattoos, and luxury items ("bling bling"); 2) level of violence, including use of knives or firearms, propensity to fighting, and threats against individuals or groups; 3) criminal activities, such as drug trafficking, pimping, fighting, or fencing stolen goods, and 4) level of involvement in gang structure, including the individual's frequency and nature of contacts with other gang members and the number of people from whom he takes orders versus the number of people to whom he gives them (figure 3, from Guay, 2007).

2

What Motivates Boys to Join Street Gangs? How Do They Become Members?

A great deal of work has been done since the 1930s on the motivations of boys who join street gangs and on their roles within gangs. Some facts are so obvious that they hardly deserve mention. Gangs are largely composed of youths from economically and socially disadvantaged neighbourhoods. Lacking better opportunities, some are easily tempted by illicit money-making schemes. Also important is that these youths generally come from visible minority communities that experience or have the impression of experiencing discrimination, exclusion, or ostracism. If they are the children of immigrants, they may be having difficulty adapting to the culture of their adoptive country, and they may have witnessed the relatively limited success of their parents and neighbours in this regard. A difficult family background may be yet another motivating factor for joining a gang.

As early as 1927, Thrasher noted that gangs emerged as accelerated immigration and urbanization gave rise to socioeconomic upheaval and social disorganization in America's large cities. They offered young people a refuge from the ghetto living conditions that were the lot of many poor people and immigrants. Cohen (1955) conceived of the gang subculture as an escape valve for youth frustrated with a society that they saw as offering unequal opportunities for success. Also of note is the theory of differential opportunities (Cloward and Ohlin 1960), in which gangs offer young people a way of attaining societally sanctioned goals using forbidden methods.

Still today, gangs form on an elective basis as a response to these conditions. Their members are united by similar experiences of personal, family, school, or relationship problems – discrimination, unemployment, unattractive job prospects, and so on. Gangs, despite their risks, hold out the promise of security, belonging, and protection from an outside world that is rightly or wrongly seen as uncertain, troubling, or threatening and at any rate a source of marginalization.

What we are saying is that prior to becoming a source of violence and intimidation, gangs are themselves a response to apprehended violence and intimidation. This fact is critical to understanding why gangs have no trouble recruiting new members. But belonging to a gang offers certain surplus benefits as well. It is often the only apparent means that these youth have of acquiring status in the eyes of their peers. When all other avenues appear to be blocked, it is the easiest way to gain "respect" and – they hope – lots of money. And then there are the girls ...

There is nothing racist or xenophobic about noticing the strikingly ethnic makeup of many street gangs. It is a simple statement of fact. Moreover, it is probably a reflection of the effects of racism and xenophobia. In both Canada and the United States, gang membership is largely composed of youth from disadvantaged neighbourhoods in which visible minorities are overrepresented. As the Chicago School sociologists of the early twentieth century pointed out, the problem does not reside in the nature of the inhabitants of these zones of poverty or transition but in their relative social disorganization (poverty, lack of community resources, lack of access to power, endemic unemployment, for example). Even academically successful visible minority youth may experience discrimination at school. They may drop out in the belief that they will never be given equal access to the labour market. They may then gravitate towards gangs for the access to wealth that they provide.

Perreault and Bibeau (2003) mention the numerous difficulties inherent in the immigration process. Families who settled in the country generations ago may still be treated as if they just arrived, causing some of their teenage members to band together out of frustration. Family breakup and differences between societal and minority cultural values may speed this process. Parents wishing to educate their children according to the principles of their culture of origin may meet with resistance and disobedience from their children, who aspire first and foremost to integrate with their adoptive society. Cohen (1955) developed his theory of delinquent subcultures based on the idea that young street gang members, mainly those from the working class, rightly or wrongly come to disqualify their parents as role models. Frustrated and angry with what they see as unequal opportunities for success, particularly at school, these youth perceive gangs as a means of escape, as the most obvious solution to their problems of integration. Moreover, as a subculture instilling new values, a gang offers opportunities for alternative forms of recognition, different from those typically valued by society.

It is true that many teenage gang members come from families with whom they no longer wish to identify. They want to do better than their parents, whose unattractive standard of living does not offer them the material goods, power, and money that the consumer society has taught them to demand. In recent decades this last point has become key to the understanding of the street gang phenomenon. While the youth observed by Thrasher in 1927 were the visible manifestation of a culture shock between the values of their communities and those of North American society, today's street gang members have largely endorsed and adopted capitalist values. For them, conspicuous consumption represents the epitome of success. The main difference with previous generations relates to the methods they adopt in order to achieve that level of consumption. For many of these young men, their parents' traditional values will no longer do. They are questing after male role models, heroes, winners; they have to succeed, and in the very short term. Gangs seem to them the perfect place to find what they are looking for: older boys who have money and success with girls and who command "respect," not only from other members but from the whole society.

Because of the felt needs that the gang meets, it comes to constitute a genuine male subculture. It becomes the quintessential setting in which virility is valued, in which boys believe they can learn what it is to be a man or how to become one by learning to inspire respect, by proving to all their physical endurance, by showing a degree of emotional insensitivity, by being highly sexually active, and by rejecting parental or institutional authority. The gang quickly becomes a second family, a chosen family, the one with which the boy proudly identifies. Being a gang member means displaying your power, and this is why it is impossible to overestimate the degree to which belonging to a gang can be a source of self-esteem for many youth who experience or fear rejection and whose life experiences, particularly in the family and at school, have offered little affirmation. They finally feel that they make a difference.

While the best-known gangs in Canada are composed of Caribbean youth (Haitian and Jamaican in particular), Latin American, Arab, and Asian gangs also exist. Police estimates for Winnipeg suggest that 85 per cent of street gang members there are aboriginals from communities in which poverty is rampant. No longer does any North American ethnic group have a monopoly on street gangs. Several practitioners in our survey noted that gangs are attracting an increasing number of "white" North American youth who feel marginalized in one way or another, thus having the effect of de-ethnicizing the composition of certain gangs.

It is no exaggeration to state that the function of gangs for their overwhelmingly male membership is to reassure and affirm them. In this connection, all of the following dynamics are at work:

- Confirmation of gender identity. The boy wants to know that he is "a man," therefore not a "girl," a weakling, or a "fag." He wants to make common cause with other young men, both peers and role models, as well as to display his physical strength and his ability to conduct "business." Finally, he must display his sexual prowess with the girls he seduces, who will "do anything" to please him.
- Ostentatious affirmation of erotic identity (heterosexuality).[7] Gang members want to be the envy of their peers by being surrounded by pretty girls, like the singers in hip-hop videos. Many videos, while presenting a rough-and-ready narrative of gang life, offer constant reminders to regard women as sex objects or whores. The young men who watch them feel their self-esteem is boosted if they are popular with women. In this they are no different from most men. And of course, youth and beauty are the female characteristics most sought after. Boys from disadvantaged groups score an especially big win if they are capable of pleasing the prettiest girls: they show that they can play to win on the same field as every other man, including the biggest "players." At the same time, gang membership makes boys heroes in the eyes

of many attractive girls, increasing their opportunities for sex with them.

- Creating a group identity. The boy thinks, "I am proud to belong to the notorious gang x." Such an identity may be made more necessary in a context where gang membership is on the rise; many boys may feel the need to protect themselves by joining a gang. Thus, gang affiliation affords a sense of safety as well as camaraderie. However, a gang can simultaneously be a site of power struggles, particularly among those who aspire to be its leaders. In short, the gang becomes a sort of second family, often more important than the family of origin.
- Instilling a social or territorial identity. Most gangs seek to control specific urban areas: a neighbourhood, a bus route, a park, a mall. They may also be associated with particular fields of illegal activity. Gangs mark their territory with visible signs such as graffiti, colours, or objects. Woe to members of another gang who ignore these warnings (which most people are not even aware of).
- Strengthening of ethnic or community identity. In many cases this helps to counterbalance societal rejection or, at least, a feeling or apprehension of being discriminated against and excluded.
- Serving as a source of income. The gang provides income through crimes such as robbery, drug dealing, prostitution, and taxing. Members can thereby acquire the identity of satisfied consumers that would otherwise be off limits to them, at least in the short term. These youth, especially the leaders, are at pains

to accumulate the things they see as marks of distinction, such as designer clothing, jewellery, luxury cars, and shows and restaurant outings. The search for immediate gratification that is said to be characteristic of youth is particularly pronounced among street gang members.

In short, it may be said that the gang generates a new order that is reassuring to its members, at least initially. For there is always the possibility (which the individual may minimize) of being caught and convicted of a crime, victimized by a competing gang, or abandoned by one's peers as a result of infighting. A boy may be left to fend for himself against his enemies. But these prospects are far from his mind when he first joins a gang. At that point it is the life he dreams of – a life of money and pretty girls.

But the gang quickly reveals its dark side as a site of legitimation of criminal behavior, which is highly esteemed by certain groups. The gang subculture shields members from feelings of guilt when they use illegal means to gain wealth and prestige. Since the group develops its own value and belief system, it encourages members to rationalize their delinquency as the only means to social success. The concept of differential access to economic and social status enunciated by Cloward and Ohlin (1960) is relevant here; boys with lesser access to status will be more inclined to use illegitimate means to attain it.

As a context of male socialization and identification, the gang values or at least legitimates even the most violent criminal behaviour. For it is also a rite of passage, a place where one goes to "take a step up," to learn to be a man (whatever that may mean for the boy in question) and, above all, to elicit "respect." Though it varies from one group to another, gang initiation most often consists of committing an act of violence against an enemy (aggression) or a civic institution (theft with vandalism) or allowing oneself to be beaten up without flinching (a rite known as a "punching initiation"). By inflicting physical suffering, the right of initiation confirms the recruit's manliness to the whole group. More crucially, the pain endured serves as proof of loyalty and complicity. The recruit is shown to be capable of inflicting the same violence on anyone he will have to intimidate, for those who have experienced violence are better able to wield it.

Physical endurance, demonstrated strength, sexual performance, rejection of authority and its laws and institutions, ability to influence or dominate others: these are some of the characteristics to which street gang members aspire. Moreover, the street, as a public space, is seen as an ideal setting in which to affirm one's manhood, contrary to the home or private space, which remains the domain of female expression – at least as generally conceived of in our culture.

In gangs, only boys and their expressions of manliness (or their idea of it) matter. Loyalty to the gang assumes that each of its members is answerable to it, literally belongs to it body and soul. This is why initiation is so often accompanied by denial of the body for the gang's benefit. The boy is willing to suffer at the hands of his colleagues, to endure their blows, not only to show that he is strong but also to show that his body and pain belongs to the gang. It is an essentially homosocial microsociety.

In summary, the gang is a boy's world, one that is imagined, created, and managed by boys. They size each other up to determine who is the strongest, the most intimidating, the most likely to create a circle of "respect" and admiration around him. For a gang ultimately rules through its ability to intimidate, beginning with its own members, then the people it seeks to control, and finally its enemies and the general public as necessary. The marginalized, fearful boy becomes the person who incites fear, completing a vicious cycle in which anyone who does not wish to be hunted becomes a hunter.

3

What Is the Status of Girls in Street Gangs?

Unlike the United States, where an increasing number of girls are joining or forming gangs, Canada is thought to have few female gang members, and most of these generally remain in the peripheral circle.[8] Machismo among gang members is one obvious explanation; another is stricter parental control over girls, whose socialization takes place more in the private sphere than in public (on the street). Girls simply have less opportunity to join a gang than do boys.

Some scholars believe that the small numbers of girls identified as gang members merely reflect the hesitancy of law enforcement personnel to identify and treat them as such. But that perception is starting to change. U.S. research over the last two decades has found that active female participation in criminal gang activities is on the rise (Taylor 1993: 10; Esbensen et al. 1999). Schalet et al. (2003: 128) noted the emergence of female-only gangs which, following the example of male gangs, are involved in prostituting other girls. Other American studies have estimated that girls represent anywhere from 20 to 45 per cent of gang members in that country.[9] The much smaller estimates for Canada reflect a distinctly different reality here.[10]

Since girls are less likely than boys to be suspected of criminal activities, their involvement can be useful in deceiving the police or the civic authorities. Therefore, gangs often use girls as accomplices in money laundering, counterfeiting, credit card theft, fencing of stolen property, and other offences. Their role tends to be that of dissimulation rather than intimidation, force, or violence (although girls are perfectly capable of these). Rarely do they command or initiate violent crimes, although they may act violently under the orders or influence of a male leader.

While the role of girls in gangs is changing, no observer of the phenomenon has any illusions that large numbers of girls will become full-fledged members. The few who achieve this status will be perceived and treated as boys, in many respects. They too will have to undergo the punching initiation and do battle with girls from rival gangs. But their femininity will never disappear altogether, far from it, and this is evident in the motives for such fights, which are frequently triggered by a perceived attack on a girl's "sexual reputation." This is of enormous importance to an aspiring female gang member. She cannot allow herself to be perceived by the boys as a mere sex object, much less a whore. To do so is to instantly lower her status to a dangerous level because of the unwritten rule whereby boys must attract and seduce girls yet show outward contempt for them. One of the most terrifying displays of this contempt is the "gang bang."

A gang bang is a ritual gang rape in which a girl is forced to have sex with several gang members at once or in rapid succession. If the same girl is subjected to more than one of these incidents, the initial one is sometimes referred to as the "sex-in." Another practice is the "roll-in," where the girl rolls a die to determine how many sexual partners she has to satisfy on the spot. Many other variations are possible.[11] One girl remembered: "My ex told me, 'We're going to see some people.' We got there and there were some guys sitting around drinking. They asked him to go get something, beer I think. As soon as he left, the guys started touching me, asking me to get undressed, telling me they wanted to 'try me.' They said, 'It's no problem, everybody's okay with it' ... I didn't know what to do. I let it happen. My ex and I never discussed it again." In another case, a new recruit was told by her female recruiter, "There's a party and you're going to be initiated. We all went through it. Just do what the guys tell you. You don't want to look like an idiot."

The main point cannot be overstressed: the gang bang is not a fun orgy but rather a purposeful assault committed by gangs that operate prostitution rings. Its main role appears to be that of sexually desensitizing both the victim and the assaulters in preparation for their respective roles in prostitution. Most obviously, it conditions the girl to have forced sex without thinking of it as rape. It is not just the traumatic bodily experience she is living through, but the simultaneous and incongruous reassurance that no trauma is being inflicted. Message: when men are having fun, you are having fun too. It does not matter what your body is telling you. The predictable post-traumatic stress symptoms the girl may experience, such as loss of sexual sensation or even a feeling of being cut off from her own body, reinforce the "normality" of submission to men's desires, however extreme, and thus create the docility that is the underage prostitute's main asset (from the pimp's standpoint, of course). She's "been there"; it's no big deal. The fear of the gang bang may itself be enough to intimidate a girl into what she sees as the lesser evil: having unwanted sex with one or more gang members, followed by paid non-consensual sex. Girls who participated in gang bangs may be reminded of their initiation with the message: you were willing to "do" anybody that night, so why turn down a paying client now? One girl recollected: "It was only later that I realized what had happened. One night I was in a bar, and all of a sudden I woke up somewhere, and all these guys were standing there expecting me to suck their dicks. I think they put something in my drink. Since that night I haven't been the same. I feel absolutely mortified."

Somewhat less obviously, the gang bang plays the role of desensitizing the boys. They cannot be allowed to nurture any feelings of love or exclusivity toward the girls whom they induct, or to resent the girls' treatment at the hands of the gang, since such feelings would limit their ability to pimp the girls without compunction. In this business, love interferes with profit margins, and so love must be vanquished by inculcating contempt. When the boys imitate their leaders (mimetism, after all, plays a pivotal role in street gangs) by "sharing" their girlfriends in a gang bang, they learn to redefine "manliness" as intense sexual desire coupled with domination of the women who allow them to fulfil it and emotional insensitivity to their needs. They enter into a pact to stand strong, as boys, against their own human emotions. An intriguing element of this pact, which we were unable to explore further in this research project, is that the act of sharing the same girl while others look on may allow the boys to have sexual feelings in male company, an experience otherwise strictly off limits in the macho world of gangs. There appears to be a homoerotic element at work here in which voyeurism and sexual promiscuity play a role.

In this way the gang bang "breaks" the boy for the role of sex slaver, just as it breaks the girl for the role of sex slave. Subsequently, as our respondents related, the gang reinforces this message by subjecting any pimp who lets a girl keep some of her earnings to ridicule and contempt. A real man must be in control, they tell him; he cannot let himself be controlled by a girl. It should be noted that by no means all boys are eager participants in the gang bang: knowing full well what lies in store for their girlfriends, they may go to great lengths to postpone the "official introduction" to the other gang members.

In short, the gang bang, like the punching initiation, puts a brand on the participants' bodies in a manner analogous to the gang's marking of geographical territory. The outward signs of allegiance (jewels, clothing, accessories, tattoos) are really only the culmination of an allegiance already more deeply inscribed in the body. The gang bang physically trains its participants, willing or unwilling, in the social and gender hierarchy by which they will be ruled and from which – so the gang leaders tell them – there is no escape.

Scholars and practitioners disagree on how common or systematic gang bangs are. Most of our respondents hold the belief that they are quite common, but each gang evidently has its traditions. Researching gang bangs is especially difficult in that many young women decline to report them. As we have seen, the acute cognitive dissonance laid over the event may lead girls to consider as group sex what was undoubtedly an instance of rape. Miller (2001) found that while all of her female respondents confirmed the existence of the practice, none admitted having participated in it. Given their depiction of it as a game, an unavoidable initiation, or a hurdle to be overcome, one wonders if they adopted the point of view of the boys who abused them. Côté (2004) found that when teenage girls were questioned by the Montreal police, even those who had participated in a gang bang did not consider it to be an instance of sexual assault. They claimed that they had consented.

Indeed, there appears to be a culture of silence among girl gang members around the phenomenon of the gang bang. No girl wants to be known as a slut, "the one who did all the boys." As well, many girls are reticent to use the term prostitution to describe their activities. Instead of using words that force them to look these experiences squarely in the face, they may think of them and describe them as survival sex: sex made necessary by the circumstances of the moment. Their core self-image is at stake, but there is more: their image in the eyes of the rest of the gang is critical to their well-being. A girl who admits the facts is simply compounding the stigma that will inevitably surround her. Instead she learns to keep her status as a sex object a secret, thus striving to maintain outward respectability and distinguish herself from the pack (Chesney-Lind and Shelden 2004).

But there are few non-sexualized positions available for girls in gangs, and these are hotly contested. Furthermore, these positions often require the girl to act as a recruiter of other girls for prostitution. Thus the dilemma: to keep her reputation intact, she must arrange for the other girls' reputations to be ruined. A dichotomy rapidly emerges between the girls who manage to preserve their sexual reputation and those who do not. The losers are doubly stigmatized: by the boys and men who exploit them and by the girls who despise them (Chesney-Lind and Shelden 2004; Schalet et al. 2003; Burris-Kitchen 1997). As a result, girl-on-girl abuse in gangs has increased (Lucchini 1996: 34), as each girl seeks to protect her sexual status by denigrating the others. Schalet, Hunt, and Joe-Laidler (2003: 117) note that the importance accorded by girls to their sexual respectability varies depending on male and female sex roles in their culture of origin. For example, sexual freedom is more widely accepted among African-Americans than Latinos.

Within the overall variation in North American gang typology, there are three general types of gangs that allow for girls' involvement.[12] Undoubtedly the most frequent type in the United States and Canada exploits girls for sexual purposes, notably prostitution (Totten 2000). The second type admits young women or girls in non-sexual roles. They have a lesser status than the boys and are generally in the minority; their main role is as accomplices in various crimes. In this context it is especially important for a girl to keep up her sexual status, since there may be opportunities for her to move from an auxiliary to a more active role (Huff 1990; Miller 1998). The third type are girl-only gangs, which tend to reproduce the culture of male gangs and may also involve victimization of other girls. No one in gang culture, whether male or female, questions the culture of machismo that reigns.

4

How Do Gangs Recruit Girls for Prostitution?

There is little consensus among observers as to the nature of prostitution in general. Some see it as a profession like any other, while others consider it an abusive and violent relationship even when it occurs between consenting adults. This debate is beyond the scope of our book. However, even the strongest partisans of adult prostitution agree that juvenile prostitution is more than an exchange of sexual services for money: it involves a form of exploitation. The law in Canada is clear on this point: anyone under the age of 18 who participates in prostitution is deemed to be non-consenting. There is no question of underage prostitution being considered a free and informed personal choice made with full knowledge of its possible outcomes and consequences.

Street gangs involved in the sex market use misrepresentation, blackmail, and coercion as recruitment strategies. As well, they use a powerful form of a technique pioneered by religious cults known as "love bombing," in which a girl is showered with affection as a means of manipulating her into doing the gang's bidding (see below). Such strategies are necessary, since few girls would likely allow themselves to be prostituted with full knowledge of what is involved; they would probably seek other solutions to their problems or needs. After all, prostitution is not a "good gig" for the girl, since the pimp (or "boyfriend," or "manager") pockets most or all of the money. She may initially see it as a way to gain power, have fun, experience excitement, or become more independent, but these goals usually turn out to be illusions.

Wherever teenage girls hang out, pimps and the girls working for them may be on the lookout for new recruits. Public and private schools, youth centres, malls, bus stations, train stations, rec rooms, concerts, video arcades, parks, sports venues, restaurants, and bars are all common recruitment sites. Experienced gangs know where to look and what to look for. They can spot a troubled runaway just hours after she has left home and offer her a welcome place to sleep. Recently, websites such as chat rooms have been used to entice girls by offering them careers as models or artists. Naïveté and the lure of glamour render them easy prey.

Since the phenomenon of street gang-controlled prostitution is underground and taboo, it is a major challenge to determine statistics such as the average age of entrance into the business. As might be expected, there is no agreement on this figure among the authors of the studies we read. Cases have been reported of girls age seven or eight working as prostitutes, but our police respondents said that these cases are extremely rare and not gang-controlled. They are a form of sexual exploitation perpetrated by adults, either individually or working as part of structured groups of pedophiles. Another point to note is that entrance into juvenile prostitution must be thought of as a process, not an event. For some girls, the gang bang is the defining moment; for others, it is the time when she has sex with her boyfriend's best friend out of a sense of duty or sympathy. Nevertheless, it is certain that girls prostituted by street gangs begin much younger than adult prostitutes, usually in early to middle adolescence rather than young adulthood.

Our interviews with practitioners suggest that pimps generally recruit teenagers over the age of fourteen, although some respondents have noted that candidates are being identified at an increasingly early age, sometimes just after primary school. By encouraging younger girls to participate in sex games, often revolving around fellatio, which is presented as ordinary, the gang works at diminishing their sexual inhibitions. It becomes normal for them to think of boys' pleasure at the expense of their own. Later, when asked to join the sex market, they will be less timid.

But the question remains: How is it that they are attracted to gangs so easily? Specifically, how can the deceptions used by pimps remain effective now that girls are increasingly aware of how they operate?[13] The answer must involve an understanding of the emotional state in which many girls find themselves. In order for them to see hanging around with a gang member and, ultimately, participation in prostitution as a solution, they must be going through a problem to which that solution responds. The ideal target is a younger girl who has run away from a problematic situation at home or school. Feeling deprived of attention and privileges, she is easily impressed by a sweet talker who promises love, the good life, or a non-stop party – all that she has ever dreamed of. She just wants to believe that she is attractive and interesting and that she has been chosen by someone who will take care of her.

Unfortunately, decades of feminism have not changed the fact that many girls' self-definition revolves around seduction and desire. Perhaps as a result, seduction is the prime strategy used by street gangs to enrol teenage girls. It is easy for them to seduce their prey by playing to their insecurity, their need for acceptance, and their emotional dependency. It is just a matter of showering them with affection – "love bombing." As necessary, the seduction will be complemented with pity, emotional gamesmanship, threats, and/or violence. After "giving his all," the pimp exploits the pseudo-love relationship, gradually becoming more demanding, coercive, and violent. Many teenage girls dream that their heart will belong to one boy, but in this case it is their body the boy is after – in order to reap its market value.

One common tactic is for a boy or a group of boys to show off their capacity to spend money, to party non-stop. For example, they may boast that they are associated with "up and coming" hip-hop groups. There is no coercion at this point, only manipulation. (Some of our respondents admitted that they are easily manipulated in just this way by the "bad boys" who run with gangs.) If the girl is receptive, the boy – her future pimp – will initiate her to gang life, beginning by showering her with gifts. He gives her jewellery and clothing and takes her to restaurants, movies, and sporting events. They go to gang parties where alcohol and drugs are generously offered. Her new circle of friends is her new family, her new culture. It is a honeymoon. She feels indebted for the material goods and attention she is getting.

The girls we interviewed stressed the insistence, persistence, and skilfulness of the seduction. "I felt like the most important girl in the world," said one. "When you're in your teens, not many boys will run after you like they do. They call you every hour. They tell you they miss you, they're thinking only of you, you're the only girl in the world. It makes an impression." What it does is to throw the girl off balance and overcome her resistance. "He wore me down with compliments," said a young woman who finally agreed to let herself be prostituted for the sake of her suddenly "broke" boyfriend. Another girl explained that she had realized what awaited her just in time, before getting into deeper trouble, and was able to escape prostitution: "When I figured out that I was far from the only one – I thought I was the only one – doing that for my boyfriend, that other girls were also doing it, it was a wake-up call. But it took me awhile to figure it out."

A reader may be tempted to respond: But these girls aren't fools! They can see what's coming. True, but many of them are deeply unhappy. They are waiting for something to happen in lives they experience as boring, unglamorous, and problem ridden. They desperately want to believe that a dream is coming true. And who can blame them if they refuse to read the signs, when the culture in which they bathe glorifies immediate gratification, while prime-time television cultivates the myth of celebrity, beauty, and instant wealth? Moreover, just as the gang gives boys an opportunity to assert a masculinity based on intimidation, violence, domination, and control, it may offer a girl an opportunity to assert a femininity based on good looks. Being seen on the arm of a gang leader may be an ego boost if she has no other way to differentiate herself. She gets to share the aura of the boy and his gang, vicariously enhancing her own importance. To girls who feel unloved by their families or experience low self-esteem, this may seem like a unique opportunity.

Even when she finds herself in prostitution somewhat later, emotional manipulation by the pimp and attention from the clients may preserve the illusion that she is seductive or possesses a certain something other girls lack. Pimps cultivate such female rivalries to their advantage. First they compliment her on her beauty, then they tell her she is losing the beauty contest and deserves no better than what she has. Disparaging remarks ("You're fat, you're old, you're ugly") allow the pimp to control the girl effectively and cheaply. As for the girls themselves, rarely is there any true friendship among them, because the pimp plays them off against each other and they will do anything to stay in his good graces. The basic rule is to show no sympathy for fellow female gang members. Fend for yourself and hold onto whatever status you can muster. The result, as many young women have recounted, is a deep feeling of isolation and loneliness. Of course, the more isolated they are, the easier they are to manipulate and intimidate.

Gangs quickly become expert at identifying a girl's particular vulnerability and using it to break down her defences. In a variant on the classic "good cop, bad cop" strategy, for example, a girl who sees herself as fat may be taunted mercilessly about her weight by the whole group. When her self-esteem is at a low ebb, along comes the good cop – an official "boyfriend" (actually, her prospective pimp), who conveys the opposite message: She is pretty, she has a great body, and if she wants to lose weight they can work out together. He is not like the others, it seems, and she falls madly in love with him.

At base, it is the desire to feel loved that leads these girls to fall under the control of gangs and stay there. As well, there is their admiration for the gang members and the easy yet exciting life they seem to lead. As long as the girl shares the gang's values and believes that her love relationship is real, she will stay under the gang's control. Many of these girls eventually perceive their willingness to be prostituted as a proof of their love for the pimp. In the words of a well-known Édith Piaf song that unfortunately reflects an ever-popular conception of love, especially among young women, "I'd do anything / If you asked me to."

Of course, this transition does not take place without a great deal of active indoctrination once the boy has gained some power over the girl. While being given glimpses of a free and independent life, she is kept psychologically and/or physically isolated from her family and background. Meanwhile, she is made to feel increasingly indebted for what she thought were "gifts" of drugs, clothing, and jewellery. The "boyfriend" dazzles her with longer-term projects such as travel, a nice apartment, marriage, or even starting a family. She is treated like a princess. But it is not long before the bill comes due: the boyfriend claims to be broke because of all the money he has spent on her, and she has to pay him back. A minimum-wage job in a clothing store will hardly serve the purpose; she can make much better money stripping or hooking. His message: "I love you, so do it for me." And so the girl rationalizes her first steps in prostitution, thinking, "After all he did for me, I owe it to him."

As soon as possible, her new boyfriend makes strenuous efforts to lower her inhibitions, so that non-reciprocal sex seems normal. He may induce her to participate in erotic games at a party, such as a striptease or a wet T-shirt contest. She may be asked to kiss and caress other girls or boys, or have sex with a lovesick "friend" in need of consolation, and then with some associates at an alcohol- or drug-fuelled party. The outcome, in some cases, is the gang bang discussed above.

Once on the sex market, the girl earns more than she ever thought possible; however, she rarely sees much of that money. The pimp claims that it is being used to pay off shared expenses or debts or that it is being set aside for future projects, including couple projects. This is obviously false, but the girl believes it for a while. Alternatively, she may be paid a percentage of the proceeds, but the pimp will try to control her bank account, seeing to it that she does not touch the money without permission. In either case, the girl is kept separate from her money. A common trick is to convince her that it is unsafe to carry money, while large bank deposits will attract the attention of her family or the authorities. She is better off letting her manager "administer" the money. She does not yet realize that the "administration fees" will cost her the bulk of her earnings and that the manager in question has two or three other girls to whom he tells the same story. This is how pimps build their business, and the amounts involved are obviously enticing to any would-be pimp who can do the math: manage a dozen girls, each making up to a thousand dollars a week, and he can get rich within a year. The actual profits in a business ruled by the law of silence are, of course, nearly impossible to quantify. It is not as though they are declared to the tax authorities! Still, the amounts at stake are evidently large enough to represent an enticing business opportunity.

Money plays a key role in the relationship between the pimp and the prostituted girl. The need for money (often to buy drugs or "luxuries") is the most frequently stated reason for girls' involvement in prostitution.[14] On the issue of drugs and prostitution, a remark is in order: the majority of Canadian studies suggest that youth involved in prostitution are generally large consumers of illicit substances. However, we do not know which is the cause and which is the effect.[15] We do know that drugs are no longer provided free of charge once the girl is being prostituted – that would be a waste. Any money she makes can be easily recaptured through drug sales. Another scam used to steal girls' money involves a legal jargon-filled "contract" between a gang and the girls it recruits. Potential "employees" who read the fine print will discover that little or no money will be left after the "manager" has taken a hefty cut for his "services."

No wonder that girls who have brought in small fortunes for their pimps often find themselves penniless several years later. Some don't even notice anything out of the ordinary, so intensely have they been brainwashed into believing that the money was never really theirs but owed to someone else. One of our respondents earns more money today working in a minimum-wage job than she did in prostitution. She remarked that pimps do nothing to deserve the pompous title of "manager" other than to make a few business calls, which the girl could easily do on her own behalf. As unreal as it sounds, some girls come to think of items bought for them with their own money as gifts. In their mind, the person who controls the money is the one to whom it legitimately belongs.

Another technique used by street gangs to recruit girls for prostitution is to use the ones they have already captured to convince friends, acquaintances, or classmates (some girls stay in school to avoid attracting the family's attention to their clandestine activities). Both Canadian and U.S. studies suggest that many girls are initiated to prostitution by other girls and not by pimps,[16] though the majority of female respondents stated that they were under the control of a pimp at one time or another. This type of recruitment often targets the notoriously vulnerable clients of foster care facilities;[17] lacking self-confidence and liable to run away, many of them can be snared with relative ease, and the first recruit may serve as a conduit to others. It is known that the names and numbers of "good guys" willing to "help" runaways are passed from hand to hand at these facilities, with predictable results.

It bears repeating, in conclusion, that girls are not attracted by prostitution as such; it is the price they find they have to pay for a boy's love and admiration. They are entrapped through seduction and the promise of a better life. For many girls, the line between a pimp and a lover is a very fine one. However, as the next section shows, the motivations of prostituted girls are multifarious.

5

What Is the Typical Profile of a Prostituted Girl?

It is never straightforward to generalize about people and behaviour. Each girl prostituted by a street gang is both similar to and different from her peers. As we attempted to understand how they think, act, and are influenced, we noticed a number of recurring themes. Some of our respondents were looking for love and found emotional dependency; others wanted easy money; still others were hungering after strong sensations and adventure. A few especially unfortunate ones had lost the capacity to decide for themselves, essentially being reduced to sex slaves. These varying motives and circumstances strongly inflected each girl's behaviour and also determined her status within the gang. To put it succinctly, each girl acted predominantly for love, for money, for a thrill, or against her will. (In some cases motives may coexist or follow one another sequentially in the same person.) In this book, we use the terms "submissives," "independents," "daredevils," and "sex slaves," respectively, as shorthand for the main groups.

The most common form is the submissive, typically a girl aged thirteen to sixteen who experiences low self-esteem, is somewhat naïve or susceptible to influence, and comes from an unhappy family background. These needy girls can quickly become emotionally dependent, and as such are unlikely to rebel against the pimp, even when they realize what they are up against. They simply submit.

Girls displaying this profile simply have no idea how wrong their "love story" is going to go. Agreeing to do everything their "boyfriend" demands, they find themselves being treated like objects or even systematically abused. By the time they identify the abuse for what it is, they are in over their heads. Some respondents reported having been assaulted by their "boyfriend" after standing up to him: "He said he didn't like being stepped to. He demanded 'respect.'" As unbelievable as it may seem, another girl recounted that her boyfriend had "sold" her to pay their debts! What she had thought to be a love relationship had turned out to be something resembling a situation of ownership and sexual slavery.

One young francophone told us how she found herself dancing in a bar many kilometres from home in an English-speaking province (her English was poor):

> My boyfriend said it was the only way to help him pay his debts. It's no fun. The clients are always touching you, reaching for your breasts, your vagina, your rectum. You have to think of something else. You have to drink or take drugs beforehand or you

just freak out. Eventually you get over it. You tell yourself it's just a massage, all those hands always touching you ... One night my boyfriend told me he had sold me to pay his debts! I didn't really know what that meant. From then on other guys were in charge of me, with other girls who worked there. A few days later, when the police checked my identity, they saw that my parents were looking for me. I had changed my age but not my name. I was panicked at being arrested. They took me to the police station and I thought I was going to go to jail, but the next day they took me home to my parents. My ex tried to get back in touch with me and I almost fell under his spell again. I was so in love with him.

Another girl told us:

I had decided to give myself all the luxuries I felt I deserved. When it came time to get into prostitution for the guy I loved, I did it. At first I was thinking I could make a bunch of money real fast and buy a car. But I had to pay percentages, I had to bring in the money, I had to do things I didn't really want to ... After years of doing that, it totally wrecked me. I'll never be the girl I was before. I'd like to leave it behind me, but when I need money I know I can always dance. It's hard not to go back to it when you're broke, or you have a dope debt, and you know you could so easily pay it off by just showing your ass.

The emotional manipulation she has undergone hinders the submissive from developing a critical awareness of her true situation. To stay in her boyfriend's good graces, she obeys his every order; completing the vicious cycle, he continues to dehumanize her. A lovestruck submissive may weather many hardships before she becomes conscious of her situation and attempts to escape. This calls for great courage, for she has witnessed the violence of which the boy and his gang are capable. She is scared, and rightly so.

Most unfortunately, some submissives are unable to exit the cycle of abuse. Under the domination of the gang, they sink to the level of sex slaves, at which point their fate is entirely out of their hands. Traumatized by their experience, terrorized by the prospect of being beaten or raped, they become zombies to themselves and subhumans to their pimps. They become property to be used as the owner sees fit, and all that matters to him is their earning power. They will be subjected to the most degrading sex acts to be found in prostitution. Once a girl has reached this status, it is extremely difficult for her to recover. Her self-esteem is gone and she is subjugated to the men who use her.

The sex slave may be sold or traded from one pimp or gang to another, as in the above-mentioned case where the girl escaped thanks to a police intervention. Her movements may be strictly controlled. In fact, she may be locked in a room and be forced to receive an unending stream of clients.

A victim recalled (describing the experience of many others), "Some of them were a lot worse off. They didn't know what was going on around them. They stopped thinking. I doubt those girls will ever get out. As long as there's a guy to take advantage of them, they're stuck." Another respondent said, "Some girls never get out. They're totally controlled by the guys and their threats and their drugs. They want to leave, but they always wind up going back. It's as if they had no other choice. Except suicide, maybe ..." A third respondent related her own experience:

> I ran away once or twice at first, but he always caught me and forced me to go back. He would punch me, pull my hair. He'd make veiled threatens about my child – it might be his – and I finally had to give the kid to my mother for safekeeping. I wound up in this cheap motel room with dirty, smelly, disgusting clients coming in all day long. Then there were the sadistic ones who took pleasure in degrading and humiliating you, treating you like a slut, forcing you to do terrible things … I threw up sometimes, it was so unbearable. When I did that I got punished. The guys [in the gang] wouldn't give me anything to eat: they would say, "That way, you won't throw up." It got to the point where I was begging – not for food but for drugs, pills, anything. The best thing that could happen was for me to forget where I was, who I was … But clients don't like it when the girls are stoned. Some of them complained about me. I won't tell you how badly I got beat up after that.

Another girl recounted, "I was pretty naïve. I had no experience. I fell in love with a gang boy; I was totally attached to him. I did whatever he told me, even having sex with four or five guys. Some of them don't smell good … I can't say I enjoyed that. At one point my boyfriend traded me. I must've gone around the whole province, certainly Montreal. I got all kinds of diseases, too: of course, nobody wants to wear a condom. I don't know if I can ever get out."

Induced drug addiction is an effective means of control: a girl who is addicted may well do anything for the sake of a fix, while many girls need one to dull the horrors of their work. Perhaps paradoxically, though, once a girl is under his control, the pimp will strictly limit her drug consumption to save money and please the clients. Also useful to the pimp in subjugating her is a background of physical or psychological abuse in the girl's life, and the fragility it brings. Many studies have confirmed that such backgrounds are typical of girls prostituted by gangs.[18]

A quite different profile emerges with the third group, the daredevils. These young women, generally older and more experienced, might be said to be active rather than passive victims. There is no need to trap them, since they voluntarily approach gangs, often through the intermediary of a friend or acquaintance. Their goals are twofold: to live the "wild life" and to make money from prostitution. Unlike the first two groups, they are not primarily interested in a boyfriend; they are looking for adventure and strong sensations. As such, they are not put off by the risks of the business. They know – or think they know – what to expect from prostitution. They generally come from more affluent (even frankly wealthy) backgrounds and usually keep a considerable percentage of their earnings. They often perceive themselves – wrongly, for reasons explained below – as full-fledged gang members. Typical comments heard from this group: "I'll save up a bunch of money and then quit"; "As long as I'm into it, I'll keep doing it."

The daredevil wants to feel like an adult woman: more sophisticated, more capable, in every way superior to the women around her. What is most important to her? Money and consumer goods,[19] beauty and seduction, the irresistible attraction of partying. An expensive drug habit is a frequent part of this picture. To the daredevil, prostitution looks like a path to material affluence and a cure for a boring, unglamorous life. It is her version of an extreme sport: risky and dangerous, yes, but all the more exciting because of it. Some of the girls involved in the rings dismantled by Operation Scorpion in Quebec City had been encouraged by their girlfriends to "go for it," to "join the gang," to brave the risks. "If you're going to have sex, why not make some money at it?" they rationalized. And once the choice was made, it was an easy matter for them to take the next step, since youth gangs are not shy about publicizing their activities. Unlike organized crime, which generally operates in great secrecy, youth gangs are highly visible in schoolyards, at recreational facilities, and around commercial establishments. They inhabit the downtown or disadvantaged neighbourhoods of many cities. They are "boys in the 'hood" and they want everyone to know it.

The daredevil believes (again, wrongly) that she knows enough about how street gangs operate to benefit from prostitution without suffering its ill effects. She thinks she is cleverer than they are, tougher than the mechanism into which she willingly inserts a finger. She can take care of herself. Said one young woman: "I had heard all the bad things about gangs. Yeah, I knew all that, but I told myself I was built tough. They couldn't beat me. I was going to take advantage of the system, not the other way around. I was a special case. It was like a game, an easy way to meet super-cool people, guys with money. But like they say, easy come, easy go. I spent all the money I made like there was no tomorrow. Restaurants, bars, fancy clothes … So I had to get up every day and do it all again. It was just … so easy."

In short, the daredevil wants to use the gang, not to be used by it. But she is guided more by recklessness and risk-taking than calculation. She minimizes the difficulties of getting away from the gang when the time comes. The gang, of course, doesn't want to lose her and will do its utmost to turn her into a submissive. Any freedom that she is allowed (in comparison with the sex slave or the submissive) will have to be earned. She may have to prove herself adept at bringing in new recruits, participating in pretty crime, laundering money, or passing counterfeit bills. She does not realize that those activities make her an easy target for blackmail when the gang needs to keep her in line. As one girl put it, "They won't let you get away so easily. Once you've worked for them, it's as if you belong to them for life. Wherever you go, whatever you do, even if you try to get out, they will come after you and threaten you and demand money. You never feel safe."

We were told that the prettier and more attractive a girl is, the more leeway she is given. She may keep a good percentage of her earnings or be allowed to frequent other gangs. If a girl secures such independence, it is largely due to her powers of attraction and seduction as perceived by the gang and the clients. Since physical appearance accounts for a great deal in the world of street gangs, a "perfect ten" has considerable bargaining power.

Girls allowed the highest level of independence constitute the group we call independents. Alternatively, they may be thought of as the subgroup of daredevils who associate with gangs while retaining maximum autonomy. But even in their case, there is never any guarantee that the autonomy will last. Financial problems, drug addiction, or a dubious love affair may put an independent on the road to submission. Daredevils and independents may be opportunistic, but the gang is equally so. And it is far from a level playing field, since gangs are expert at identifying others people's weaknesses.

The independents recounted that prostitution is a way for them to earn easy money as needed, and only then. For them the gang is a source of "contacts." In addition to hooking, they may participate in the gang's criminal activities as recruiters, informers, shills, or lookouts. Since they are not closely tied to any one gang, they sometimes serve as spies between rival gangs.

A young independent who contacted us as a respondent comes from a wealthy but troubled family, and she started running away from home in her early teens: "I got into prostitution, but I never got locked into a gang. I was mistrusting by nature, so I would just go home. I didn't run away to have someone else tell me what to do! ... I was one of the prettiest girls. I could draw clients just by walking into a bar. The guys in the gang respected me and sometimes referred me clients. In return, I told them about girls who might be interested in working." Today this young adult is a dancer in a bar while planning to continue her studies. "I'll go back to school when I'm not as hot," she admits. She has no pimp but has to pay the bar and its staff in order to work.

A point should be emphasized here. Although they are a small minority as compared with the submissives and the sex slaves, the daredevils and especially the independents serve as living advertisements for the life of prostitution. They have money, they have freedom, they are well-dressed; perhaps they have their own apartment and car. To new arrivals and prospects, their lives look highly attractive. They are an example of the "showcase effect." Like department store showcases, the independents' role is to bring in "customers," in this case the teenage prospects who are looking for a place in the sun.

In summary, the profiles of prostituted girls can be depicted with a concentric circle diagram similar to the one used to describe gang members themselves (figure 4).

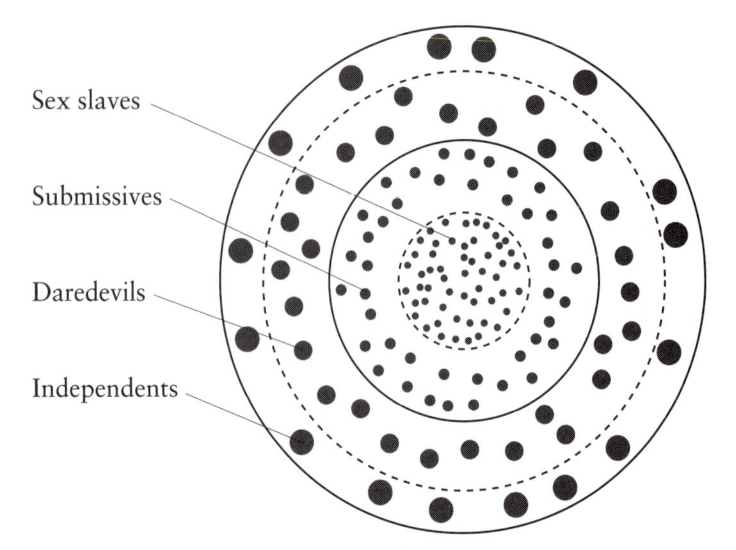

Figure 4 Circle diagram of young sex workers

This diagram is not intended to quantify or reflect the prevalence of these categories, merely to present a spectrum ranging from most to least gang control over the girls. Such quantification is impossible, particularly since the numbers of daredevils and independents, who have less interaction with social services and the police, are likely to be underestimated.

In the inside circle are the submissives, the girls who went into prostitution for love. Some of these slip into the innermost circle of sex slavery, losing all power over their lives. In the outer circle are the daredevils, who generally retain some freedom since they have consented to prostitution (or at least to their idea of it). Unlike the first two groups, they often keep some of their

Motives	Sex slaves	Submissives	Daredevils	Independents
For love	+	+ +	–	– –
For money	– –	–	+	+ +
Under coercion	+ +	+	–	– –
For adventure	– –	–	+ +	+

Figure 5 Motives of young sex workers

earnings and are valued by the gang leaders, especially if they recruit "new blood" for the ring. On the periphery are the independents, who appear to have total freedom. For them, prostitution is a business, just as it is for the gang, and the two carry on what is essentially a business relationship. The table above (figure 5) summarizes the profiles of these four groups of girls. It bears repeating that they are not mutually exclusive; a girl may fit more than one profile at different times.

For submissives and sex slaves, the main motivation is the search for love. This leads them into emotional dependency on the pimp, who controls them at will. The promised monetary benefits do not materialize. For daredevils, the main motivations are thrill-seeking and money. The independents share these motivations but exert much more control over the interaction. They may face coercion, but on nothing like the same level as submissives and sex slaves.

Thus, the situation in gang-controlled juvenile prostitution is more diverse than one might assume, in some respects subtly varied, in others starkly contrasting. However, the practitioners we interviewed left no doubt that submissives and sex slaves account for the majority of prostituted girls. Their assessment may be biased to some extent; after all, their work brings them into contact with girls who have been severely victimized by their experience with street gangs, whereas daredevils and independents do not see themselves as victims. Still, these girls are playing with fire. Their status can change if they are not careful, since gangs have every interest – most importantly, a substantial financial interest – in subjugating them.

Our research, confirmed by others (Molidor 1996; Nixon et al. 2002), shows that female juvenile prostitution in North America is often a highly controlled, coercive enterprise. As we have seen, the relationship between the girl and the pimp is generally typified by emotional dependency, intimidation, exploitation, violence, and restricted movement.

6

What Are the Characteristics of Street Gang-Controlled Prostitution Rings?

While not all street gangs operate prostitution rings, many studies affirm that such rings are now a typical part of their criminal repertoire (Blondin 1995; Grégoire 2001; Knox 2004; Cousineau 2004; Baraby 2005). Unlike drugs or stolen property, a girl can be repeatedly prostituted or "sold." For pimps, she is walking cash register. Yet despite their designation, street gangs are not frequently involved with street prostitution of the kind practised by adult women and by boys.[20] Indeed, several studies (Lowman 1987; Shaver 1996; Parent and Bruckert 2005) have shown that many adult female prostitutes do not have procurers (although they may have to pay the criminal group in control of their neighbourhood for the right to stand on a street corner). More to the point, gangs cannot readily prostitute girls on the street, since they would be quickly spotted by the police. It would also be harder to control their movements and their relations with clients.

The main activities of interest to street gangs are nude dancing (in full-service or "FS" clubs allowing "extras," i.e., sex, during or after the dance) and prostitution through certain escort agencies. Some specialists think that gangs mostly shun minors because of the police scrutiny they are bound to attract. Others disagree, arguing that minors are prized for their vulnerability to manipulation and intimidation. At any rate, the likelihood of a police raid is greatly lessened by the girls being generally offered to clients in clandestine locations such as an apartment, hotel or motel room, or backstore area. They may be allowed to go to the homes of trusted clients if the gang is sure it will not lose control over them. Rural strip bars and their adjoining motels or rooming houses are an even more convenient venue for the pimps. Confederates working there can keep them apprised of the girls' movements, while police surveillance is less intense. Several of our respondents reported being confined in situations like these and forced to service any client who showed up, on pain of food (or drug) deprivation or beatings. The more private the location, the tighter the control, and the less likely the police are to discover it. In this way, isolation increases the danger of violence.

Girls working on the street or in a club are contacted directly by the client. Pimps (or delegated male or female gang members) keeps an eye on them, less in order to "protect" them than to keep tabs on their earnings. Girls working in a room or through an agency are connected with clients through ads placed by the pimp in certain newspapers, or – much safer and more discrete – by word of mouth. The ad stresses the girl's underage status in euphemistic terms that any potential client can readily grasp. The pimp's main working tool is the telephone, over which the price, place, and "goods" are agreed upon. Some "regulars" always meet the same girl under the same conditions; most apparently make specific demands as to the girl's appearance, docility, or performance. Telephone numbers of prized girls are passed around among regular clients and their acquaintances.

Unlike the clients of adult prostitutes, men who prefer teenage girls tend to form clandestine networks of initiates. They know full well that their activities are illegal, so this secretive *modus operandi* becomes necessary to avoid police and public scrutiny. Even their close friends or relatives may not know what they are up to. The networks allow them to exchange tips about "new arrivals" and how to avoid trouble with the girls, their pimps, their relatives, and the police. The more experienced men become procurers themselves of a sort (a finding of the Operation Scorpion crackdown), and may exhibit the sociological profile of "career clients." Being a regular client, after all, requires a degree of knowledge or competency. The man must know where and how to find girls, how to negotiate the price of a session, how to demand certain sexual services, how to avoid being caught by the police or targeted for blackmail, and so on. This competency is developed over a period of several years and through contact with the network. It is then passed on to new initiates.

Some remarks are in order about the production of child pornography, which has been linked to juvenile prostitution.[21] Due to the connections between organized crime and street gangs, girls under gang control are at risk of being coerced into pornography, and this phenomenon has been reported by girls as young as thirteen or fourteen. It is said to be growing rapidly, but it is difficult to patrol and even more difficult to investigate, and its precise extent is unknown.

These images are largely distributed through electronic channels: peer-to-peer (P2P) networks, Usenet newsgroups, websites, e-mails, IRC chat networks, and so on. Cyberangels, an online education and safety program, estimated the number of pedophilic sites at thirty thousand in 1999,[22] and all observers agree that the number has increased dramatically since then (Thornburg and Lin 2002; Jenkins 2001). Rettinger (2000: 11), reviewing several studies, found that most of this material was of the "homemade" type, but this certainly does not exclude the possibility that gangs could have had a hand in producing it. For example, some of the teenagers involved in the sex rings dismantled by Operation Scorpion were forced by gang members to make live Internet pornography.

An ongoing study by one author of this book and his research team (Corriveau and Fortin, forthcoming) has found that pornographic images involving children are largely traded among networks of "discriminating consumers" through newsgroups, mostly Usenet, though new channels are being used as well. In addition, there is a grey area between undeniably pedophilic images (prepubescent children) and those that stress the juvenility of the "model," who may be a young adult. Illegal pornography is also distributed over commercial websites.[23] The Internet is rife with suggestive invitations to visit other sites where the individuals are "younger," "barely legal," "preteen," or "virgins." These sites are notable for the large number of miscellaneous keywords under which they are indexed in search engines. The result may be to hide illegal material such as child pornography, sex tourism, and prostitution in a vast network of legal adult pornography. However, there is no sure way of determining whether the girls exhibited in these images are older adolescents or young adults.[24] Certain adult pornography may be illegal under Canadian law for other reasons, especially if it contains scenes of violence such as rape or incest. This phenomenon is of great concern because these images involve real violence and real suffering. They are horror films without special effects.

For some practitioners, the context and sense in which certain girls use the word "sold" points to the existence of genuine sex slavery in Canada. The term "white slave trade" often used to describe such a phenomenon, is not, of course, a reference to skin colour: it applies to anyone who participates in prostitution against her will. It happens that (to our knowledge) a majority of prostituted girls in Canada are white, as is only to be expected in a white majority society. It is possible that girls from ethnic groups making up the bulk of certain gangs' membership are more aware of the dangers and more distrustful of the promises.

As we have indicated above, we agree that some girls' accounts display the hallmarks of sex slavery. This is not a metaphor. When a teenage girl is locked in a room, forced to have sex with strangers, and paid no money for her pains, and when pimps can acquire the right to treat her this way through an exchange of money or services, the primary meaning of the word "slave" becomes perfectly appropriate. However, this view is not unanimously held. Some practitioners counter that no real traffic in human beings is taking place. They claim that when a girl is sold, it merely means that her affiliation has changed from one group to another.

Nevertheless, traffic in human beings for sexual purposes has come under increasing law-enforcement scrutiny in recent years. This phenomenon is associated in the public mind with Third World sex tourism, but it exists and may be expanding in North America. Certain practitioners believe that street gangs are actually involved in "exporting" girls out of Quebec and "importing" them from elsewhere. New arrivals in Canada are especially vulnerable in that they may have no legal existence in this country. Time will tell whether these deeply troubling speculations are borne out.

In conclusion, there are obstacles aplenty to obtaining accurate data on the magnitude and nature of street gang-controlled juvenile prostitution rings: the secrecy surrounding them, the clients' anonymity, the girls' fear of reprisals if they seek help, their distrust of adults and institutions, and the gaps in practitioners' knowledge about the phenomenon.[25] As juvenile prostitution is an underground market, its absolute dimensions are impossible to assess accurately. Even many of the girls in question do not know for whom they are working. As for the clients, they ask no questions, pay their money, and disappear. Whatever their special desires – S&M? a threesome? an "orgy" with a group of girls? – the underage sex market will go to great lengths to fulfil them. Discretion guaranteed, cash only.

7

Who Are the Clients of Juvenile Prostitution? Why Are They Interested in Minors?

The client represents the hidden face of juvenile prostitution. Some studies take such a single-mindedly supply-side approach that the client falls out of the picture: prostitution exists simply because girls and pimps have a service to provide. Yet it is obvious to anyone that this market is largely demand driven: no one is forcing men to seek out sex with underage girls.

For pimps and prostituted girls, a client is a "trick": basically, a wallet on legs, someone to take maximum advantage of because he is willing to spend money for sex. This is an enigma to many pimps, who can have sex with girls for free: ("Those geezers must be really hard up!") The girls, too, have no respect for these men – understandably: most of the clients think only of their own pleasure and treat the girls like objects.

As for the clients, they have no illusions about the commercial nature of the transaction. They know that the pimps and the girls just want their money: no money, no candy. The candy, of course, is a docile girl who accedes to the client's sexual demands and pretends to like it – "a little slut," in the typical phrase used by the men. It is indicative of the way they perceive the relationship, the subjugation that characterizes it and, in some cases, the sadistic treatment they intend. A girl learns this in short order, while also discovering that her own needs are diametrically opposed: "The faster he comes, the better, as far as I was concerned," said one respondent. "The best client is a premature ejaculator." Of course, "nice" clients do exist, according to the accounts of some of these young women. But ultimately, a "nice" client is just one who is less demanding than the others.

Not much research has been done in Canada or the United States on clients, and none at all, to our knowledge, on the clients of prostituted girls. The methodological obstacles to such a study are enormous, beginning with the fact that clients are hard to identify unless they are arrested (Lowman and Atchison 2006). There is simply no way to define or take a representative sample of a study population that jealously guards its anonymity. However, inquiries into underage prostitution by UNICEF (2001) and the Conseil du Statut de la Femme du Québec (2002) concluded that nothing appears to distinguish clients of underage girls, as a group, from the clients of adult prostitutes. Therefore, in what follows, we derive whatever insight we can into our subject from studies of the latter group.

A recent study ventured that 12 per cent of French men use the services of adult prostitutes (Legardinier and Bouamama 2006). In the United States, Monto (2000) mentions the National Health and Social Life Survey of 1992, which estimated that 16 per cent of men have used prostitution at least once and that 0.6 per cent do so at least once a year. We are unaware of any similar studies for Quebec or Canada. The recent report of the Subcommittee on Solicitation Laws of the House of Commons Standing Committee on Justice and Human Rights, titled *The Challenge of Change* (2006), confirmed that little is known about prostitution clients in Canada except for the obvious fact that they are almost exclusively men arrested for soliciting sexual services.[26] It may be inferred that this data is skewed toward men of more modest incomes, since clandestine juvenile prostitution is beyond the means of all but wealthier individuals.

According to a review of available data by the Conseil du Statut de la Femme (2002), the typical profile of a client, irrespective of his tastes or interests, is that of a married father aged thirty-five to fifty. The practice is common to men from all socioeconomic classes who can afford to indulge in it. Mansson (1986) found that a majority of 170 clients who responded to his survey were in their thirties, 47 per cent had a stable relationship with a woman, and 70 per cent were occasional users of sexual services. In another study (Legardinier and Bouamama 2006), 36 per cent of eighty-nine respondents were over fifty, while 46 per cent were in their thirties or forties; 52 per cent were fathers, and 63 per cent were not in a couple although 71 per cent had been at one time. A third study (Dufour 2005) found that two-thirds of sixty-four respondents had been or were still married and nearly 50 per cent were fathers aged thirty-six to fifty-five. On the whole this corroborates work done in Canada since the mid-1980s, although in Lowman and Atchison (2006), 54 per cent of respondents were single. In the United States, Busch, Belle, Hotaling and Monto (2002) and Monto and McRee (2005) reached similar conclusions: the typical client is a well-educated white heterosexual man in his late thirties who holds a full-time job. In short, the average client is the average man.

A series of qualitative studies focusing on Quebec City (Dufour 2005), the United States (Monto 2000, 2004; Monto and McRee 2005), Vancouver (Lowman and Atchison 2006), Australia and New Zealand (Holzman and Pines 1997), Sweden (Mansson 1986), and France (Bouamama 2004) sheds light on clients' expressed motivations for seeking out adult prostitutes. An important caveat: this research generally takes the interviewees' statements at face value; it does not try to probe their psychology to determine "what they really meant." But since participation in prostitution exposes the men to public scorn, they may well be prone to self-justification, for which the reader of the study will have to correct. To a client, there are always fine and noble reasons to become a client.

Dufour (2005) interviewed sixty-four clients and performed a content analysis of their stated motivations for seeking out prostitutes. On this basis, she grouped them into five categories: insatiable, dissatisfied, timid, chronically unattached, and "secretive," a euphemism for men who want fetishistic or sadomasochistic relations. (There is undoubtedly some overlap between these categories; one man may well be a timid, insatiable, dissatisfied bachelor looking for very specific sexual experiences.) The majority of respondents expressed feelings of loneliness. Though many were in couples, they had difficulty finding women who would meet their expectations. The majority (56.2 per cent) ranked casualness as the most attractive aspect of prostitution. They rejected the constraints of male-female relationships but refused to go without sex. A substantial minority (38.6 per cent) considered prostitution as a stopgap until they could find a regular sexual partner.

Mansson (1986) found that clients mentioned three main motives for going to prostitutes: 1) sex without commitment; 2) loneliness (not as common; most clients had one or even several consensual partners at the time of the interview); and 3) compensation for a dissatisfying couple life. Mansson noted that fantasies about prostitutes played a larger role in the client's arousal than the sexual interaction itself. Holzman and Pines (1997) reached similar conclusions; their respondents frequently reported being aroused by the illicit and risky nature of the relationship. This remark is especially pertinent to an understanding of the demand for juvenile prostitution.

In Canada, Lowman found that 15 to 20 per cent of clients were primarily looking for affection and only secondarily for sex.[27] In the same vein, many adult sex workers testified to the House of Commons Standing Committee on Justice and Human Rights (2006) that they offer services to clients who suffer from major handicaps or difficulties socializing with women and would not otherwise have access to sexual intimacy. Problems with socializing also emerged as a major factor in the study by Monto (2000). Of eighty respondents arrested for soliciting sex workers on the street, 42 per cent considered themselves too timid to talk to a woman, 23.4 per cent found it difficult to meet women other than sex workers, and 23.3 per cent considered themselves insufficiently physically attractive. Of the group, 19.3 per cent "would rather have sex with a prostitute than have a conventional relationship," 29.1 per cent "didn't want the responsibilities of a conventional relationship," and 33.3 per cent "didn't have time for a conventional relationship." Still, sexually assertive motives were the most common: "I like nasty women" (53.9 per cent); "I'm excited by the idea of approaching a prostitute" (46.6 per cent); "I like to have a variety of sexual partners" (44.1 per cent); "I want a different kind of sex than my regular partner wants" (42.6 per cent). Monto concluded that clients' motivations are multiple and highly variable.

Quite similarly, Bouamama (2004) and Legardinier and Bouamama (2006) identified five recurring motives among their French respondents: 1) unbearable loneliness; 2) distress, fear, or frustration with women; 3) belief in an irrepressible male urge requiring immediate satisfaction; 4) refusal to commit; and 5) psychological addiction to prostitution.

The French researchers found that clients tend to trivialize and normalize their use of prostitution. Most of them adamantly rejected the characterization of clients as "dirty old men" or perverts, and took particular exception to being described as pedophiles (even if they preferred very young women). Some thought of themselves as the victims of "inaccessible," "selfish," or "complicated" women or of their own history of sexual unhappiness. They were at pains to distinguish between ordinary, reasonable clients, with whom anyone could identify, and mentality ill, dangerous, or violent clients, whom none of them had ever met. To listen to their accounts, it is as if clients as a group are a sort of "nice guys' club" – a limited, not to say idyllic perception of the conditions under which prostitution happens. A similar conclusion was reached by one author of this book in a previous work on child prostitution (Dorais 1987).

Self-justification indeed abounds in the discourse of these clients. There is always a good reason to seek out a prostitute (in this case an adult woman). Lowman and Atchison (2006) reported that 27 per cent of their eighty respondents claimed to have purchased sexual services spontaneously, while 41 per cent stated that they had been induced to use them by the availability and/or of visibility of sex workers. While this smacks of a convenient rationalization, it may indicate the need for a prudent revision of the idea that prostitution is strictly demand driven. Lowman and Atchison write, "Like most other goods and services bought and sold in a consumer society, demand and supply interact: for a certain segment of the sex buyer population, their initial demand was, at least partly, supply-driven."

While we did not interview clients for our research, we did examine some of the defence arguments that they put forward in the courtroom. On the whole, they claimed to be "nice guys" who meant no one any harm. A few even contended that they had been taken advantage of by a seductive, "surprisingly mature" girl who had lied about her age. Others presented themselves as patrons or educators of girls in need of love, paternal advice, or money. Paying for sex, in their eyes, was a favour that they had granted, not one that they had received. Yet another defence adduced on the stand was a "love of women" so irrepressible that it had impelled the man to pay for sex.

These data, observations, and accounts illustrate the strategies used by clients of prostitutes (including minors) to rationalize conduct that is beyond the pale for the rest of society. Among others, they put the best face on their motives ("I'm helping her pay her debts"), blame the victim ("She lured me"), deny personal responsibility ("My sexual urges are uncontrollable"), or trivialize the offence ("Society and the justice system are making a fuss over nothing"). Simultaneously, they deny awareness of the harms caused by prostitution. The girls' ordeal or trauma, even if a direct result of the clients' behaviour, comes as a total surprise to them. Few clients appear willing to admit the undeniable fact that what prostitutes feel for most of their clients is disgust, not desire. No surprise there: very few people, including most clients, however "insatiable," could bear up under a long series of non-consensual sexual encounters, day after day, not to mention that many of the men are as old as the girl's father or grandfather. (The bitterness of this experience showed in our respondents' repeated characterization of clients as "geezers" or "perverts.") There are limits to what anyone can endure, but to think about that is to court feelings of guilt, and guilt kills erotic desire. At best, the client of a prostituted girl cultivates his blindness to her ordeal by fantasizing that he's the only one; at worst, he abuses her, knowingly taking advantage of her fragility, inexperience, and fear.

In the absence of specific data on the clients of prostituted girls, we put forward here some likely factors stoking the demand for their services. One is society's obsession with pedomorphism, otherwise known as the altar of the youthful, sexy body at which both older women and prepubescent girls are commanded to worship. This leads many men to focus their erotic desires on considerably younger and more slender partners. Is this a natural phenomenon, as biologists and sexologists are apt to contend, or a cultural fact, as sociologists such as ourselves are inclined to believe? Certainly the culture of consumerism, with its enormous emphasis on youth and the body, accentuates the phenomenon. The canons of female beauty are intimately bound up with youth, which is why a growing number of older women are willing to pay so much for cosmetics and surgery.

Another societally conditioned impulse found in certain men is the eroticization of the forbidden. Most of the major religions and the cultures in which they are rooted place taboos on a great many sexual acts and situations. While the taboo acts as a barrier for many individuals, it provokes a transgressive reaction in others. The act of breaking the taboo is infused with erotic significance and becomes a source of arousal. In sexually jaded individuals, an escalation may occur, where the client moves from adult to juvenile to child prostitutes in an attempt to relieve boredom or add "spice" to his life. From what we know, a taste for the forbidden applies to the choices of partners and the sexual activities of clients of prostituted girls.

There is a term for the specific desire for adolescents: hebephilia. Hebephilia is the sexual attraction to youths who are pubescent but not fully developed or mature in physical and psychological terms. Pedophilia, in contrast, applies to persons sexually excited by prepubescent children, generally under the age of twelve. Hebephilia may be exclusive (the person is only attracted to adolescents), preferential (the person is mainly attracted to adolescents but not to the exclusion of other partners), or occasional. It is just as reductive to believe that a client of prostituted girls is necessarily a pedophile (although pedophilia and hebephilia can coexist in one person) as to consider him beyond suspicion simply because he has, or has had, adult partners.

Nevertheless, it seems clear that many men who turn to minors for sex are motivated by a will to control, dominate, or even degrade others. For these men, the girls' status as minors is not incidental. It is indispensable if they are to experience the forbidden, or to dominate a more vulnerable person, or simply to obtain sexual services that adult sex workers would likely refuse: sex without a condom, sadomasochism, or violent or humiliating acts, for example. A docile girl who is already under a street gang's control serves these purposes much better. In general, these clients orchestrate and control the encounter for these purposes.

The myth of an uncontrollable male urge has long been used by sexual abusers and rapists of children to justify their actions. But it is now generally accepted that nothing forces anyone to give in to his urges, however conformist or bizarre they might be. Life in society is a long process of learning to manage frustration, in sex as in any other area of life. Everyone must learn to say no to themselves and to take no for an answer. Yet a certain idea of recreational sex persists, a vision in which it has no consequences, at least for its "consumers." In this respect, the conceptions of pimps and clients coincide: girls exist not for themselves but for the pleasure and benefit of men.

In closing this section, a comment on the judicial treatment of clients is in order. The main recommendation of the practitioners and victims we interviewed is to increase maximum sentences for clients of prostituted girls. Most of these respondents doubt that fines or community work are sufficient to deter clients from recidivism. Taking sexual advantage of underage girls, they insist, is a sign of personal or relational problems that probably demand professional help. Probationary sentencing requiring clients to get help controlling their inclination for minors should be the rule (although therapeutic methods in this area stand to be greatly improved). Unfortunately, the courts still operate as if the fact of paying for sexual services from minors mitigates the offence. According to this mercantile logic, a client found guilty of abusing a teenager will get a much lighter sentence than any other person – a father, uncle, teacher, or trainer, for example – who does likewise.

8

Why Is It So Difficult to Dismantle Juvenile Prostitution Rings?

Prostituting minors is a high-risk activity. Street gangs know this all too well, especially after the crackdowns in recent years. Some consider it a matter of basic precaution to move full-time prostituted girls to another city, where they will not be recognized by relatives or neighbours and cannot get in touch with them in a situation of distress. In Quebec, moving a young francophone to an English-speaking region further isolates and destabilizes her.

Another factor hindering the fight against juvenile prostitution is that street gangs operate for the most part as relatively autonomous cells – a bit like terrorist cells – and not according to a formal hierarchy as is typical of criminal biker gangs or mafias. It is harder to identify who does what and who controls whom. Each gang member has as many as a dozen girls under his responsibility. The gang itself is not "responsible" for the acts – only one (or two or three) of its members are. Still, the pimp receives help from his associates or from members of other criminal organizations. He needs them to watch or house the girl, or to put her to work in escort agencies or strip bars far from her home. It takes a number of people to oversee the prostitution of one girl, so it is difficult, even for the girl in question, to know who exactly is profiting from her work. For example, a pimp may tell a girl that he is taking her to a city where he has "sold" her, but how can she verify the truth of this or find out whether most of the money is still going to the same person? Some young women who have been reduced to sex slaves simply no longer know to whom they "belong"– all they know is that they must keep bringing in the money.

The shifting composition of gangs and their activities makes police work particularly complex. Due to the young age of their members and, in some cases, their ethnic origin, gangs are more difficult to infiltrate than traditional criminal organizations. Moreover, it is easier for them to terrorize girls and their friends and relatives so that their activities remain a secret.

Finally, and most regrettably, the extent and even the existence of juvenile prostitution are often questioned or trivialized. There is a crying lack of awareness on the part of social workers and police officers at all levels of the hierarchy as well as on the part of Crown prosecutors and judges. As many of our respondents suggested, this gap must be filled with continuing education, especially given how diverse and complex street gangs and their pimping activities may be. They will carry on with those activities, even if we close our eyes to the problem. And, since secrecy is their main asset, acknowledging their existence and understanding how they operate can only be disadvantageous to them.

9

How Are Street Gangs Linked to Organized Crime?

Exploiting people's guilty pleasures has always been a profitable business for all kinds of criminals, organized and otherwise. During Prohibition, the clandestine production, importation, and sale of alcohol made colossal fortunes for the suppliers. Prostitution, particularly in situations where it allows clients to transgress taboos, has always been a lucrative market. Street gangs did not invent juvenile prostitution, but they changed the conditions under which it takes place. Their recruitment methods, drawing heavily on seduction, enable them to attract girls who would never otherwise have considered prostitution. What is more, the gangs surround the business with an aura of glamour, at least in certain communities, depicting prostitution as an acceptable activity for any girl who is in love with a gang member or seeking an adventure.

The crackdown on organized crime in Quebec a few years ago (particularly Operation Spring 2001, against criminal biker gangs) created a vacuum of sorts in the drug and prostitution markets. There was room for new blood. Neither the biker gangs nor the other traditional mafias gave up their hard-won control over their territories, but the police have noticed changes in the activities and alliances of street gangs. While not long ago youth gangs were mainly involved in taxing in the schools and drug dealing to adolescents, their involvement in juvenile prostitution and drug trafficking is no longer in doubt. Criminal Intelligence Service Canada (CISC 2003) still hesitates to consider street gangs as structured criminal organizations, yet many such gangs undeniably meet the two defining criteria of section 467.1(1) of the Criminal Code:

1 The group is composed of three or more persons in or outside Canada.
2 The group has as one of its main purposes or main activities the facilitation or commission of one or more serious offences that, if committed, would likely result in the direct or indirect receipt of a material benefit, including a financial benefit, by the group or by any of the persons who constitute the group.

In Quebec, a decision by Judge Jean-Pierre Bonin in January 2007 in the case of the Pelletier street gang in Montreal found five gang-linked defendants guilty of participation in a criminal organization, holding that their gang met the section 467.1 definition. This precedent should allow the Canadian police and courts to change their methods for dealing with street gangs. Even before this decision, however, it was known that street gang members had become associated with traditional organized crime (usually in the role of subordinates). Street gangs are useful to traditional organized crime in that they can buffer it from the general public. After years of bloody skirmishes and high-profile trials, these criminals are anxious to retire from the limelight. They are delighted that the focus has shifted away from them and onto street gangs.

By contracting out prostitution and drug dealing, organized crime now has the best of both worlds. It has publicly washed its hands of its most socially unacceptable criminal activities while privately continuing to derive income from them, thanks to the protection money paid by gang members to operate on their territories. Certain police sources believe, however, that one element of organized crime (especially prevalent among biker gangs) is not favourable to the prostitution of minors and tends to close its eyes to the phenomenon rather than actively encourage it.

According to our police respondents, one of the most evident aspects of collusion between street gangs and organized crime in juvenile prostitution relates to the fact that organized crime "tolerates" gang-exploited minors working under false pretences (forged papers, faked identity, lying about age) in strip clubs that it controls or "protects." Bars in rural areas, being less closely watched by the police, are ideal locations to hide adolescents and put them to work. In exchange for this service, the criminal organization receives an initial payment. The bar owner or operator subsequently collects a share of that girl's earnings. One young woman told us that after paying her dancing fee, the bar percentage, the mandatory DJ and bouncer tips and, of course, her "manager's" share, she was left with just enough money to buy the drugs she needed to carry on.

All these people profit from this system. Traditional organized crime benefits by publicly keeping a distance from unpopular criminal activities while continuing to take a cut on them. Meanwhile, the gangs prosper. Their members bear the risks of being arrested and prosecuted in return for a share of the profits. And since their shadowy structure (or rather, their lack of formal structure) makes them difficult to dismantle, both parties come out winners. Finally, if any friction should arise between them, organized crime still has the muscle to bring the gangs into line.

Some gang members are so proud of their success in prostitution that they tattoo the number 212 – the section of the Criminal Code making soliciting a crime – on their own or the girls' bodies; it also appears in the graffiti they spray on buildings in areas they control. Provided it remains out of the public eye, prostitution of minors is one of the least risky criminal domains, and unlike drug dealing, it requires almost no initial investment.

Gang-linked prostitution rings in Quebec City were destabilized at the cost of a very extensive police investigation, aided by the fact that some of the girls involved also worked for a small ring operated out of legitimate storefronts. They were under no physical constraints, kept their earnings, and on the whole considered themselves much better treated than gang-controlled prostitutes. As such, they were not as terrorized as the others and better able to testify against the pimps and the clients. Most of the clients arrested and prosecuted had done business with that ring and not with the street gangs. Thanks to the assistance of citizens and victims, the police nonetheless rounded up gang members, many of whom were convicted and sentenced to prison terms. These arrests reminded the gang members that pimping, especially where it involves minors, is an offence punishable by imprisonment. Unfortunately, the clients got off with fines or community service. Meanwhile, the gangs can claim to the clients that they never violated the law of silence in regard to their business relationship, which can now continue relatively unimpaired.

The most insidious effect of the pact between street gangs and organized crime is the increasing trivialization of the sexual exploitation of minors. While certain elements of organized crime were once reticent to encourage child or teenage prostitution, the arrival of street gangs on the scene has imposed a new order. At best, the criminal organizations tolerate them and close their eyes; at worst, they profit from the new source of wealth represented by large-scale sexual exploitation of girls. More than ever, money has no odour, colour, or morality.

10

Why Is It Hard for Girls to Testify against Pimps and Clients?

Quebec City's Operation Scorpion, which led to several prosecutions, showed how difficult it is to obtain ironclad evidence against clients and pimps and, in particular, to establish the credibility of the victims' testimony. Considering and treating these girls as ordinary witnesses seems particularly counterproductive.

Prostitution, especially in the context of intimidation and violence that characterizes street gangs, causes genuine trauma in many girls, compounding the hurt caused by their difficult family background. While it is relatively easy to fall into the trap of gang-controlled prostitution, it is much harder to get out. It depends on the gang and the pimp. Some boast that they have so many recruits that nobody needs to stay against her will, but this statement can certainly be taken with a grain of salt. There is no doubt that many girls have been repeatedly threatened, intimidated, beaten, or raped. Some live in fear for their lives.

If a pimp loses a girl under his control, especially one of the sex slaves who service his clients without respite, he loses a small fortune. Faced with the threat of violent coercion, she may agree to relations that cause deep emotional wounds if not physical ones; after all, most girls' bodies are not designed to withstand the continual impact of adult male bodies, many of them rather corpulent. In addition, the physical or sexual relations demanded may be degrading or violent in and of themselves: repeated and painful instances of sodomy, coprophagy, urolagnia, and other sadistic acts. It is no surprise that many of these girls experience post-traumatic stress disorder. If adult women abused in prostitution have been shown to experience this disorder (Farley et al. 1998), it stands to reason that teenage girls would exhibit an even more intense form of it.

One of our respondents told us she has frequent panic attacks and memory flashes of rapes at the hands of the gang and the clients. She had left the gang sometime ago but was still haunted by memories of terrible sensations and scenes: "I sleep terribly, I wake up in a panic, as if it had just happened, or as if it was just about to happen. I can't control it. It's as if the more things go, the more it comes back. If I try to repress it, it just comes back in all these weird forms. It's scary."

Such post-traumatic stress symptoms, it should be noted, frequently occur after individuals experience events during which their or a loved one's integrity is seriously threatened, or they feel intense fear associated with impotence, an inability to escape the situation.

Invasive memories of moments of distress may then come back to haunt them, as if the situation were about to reoccur, particularly under circumstances evoking the dramatic event. To cope with these extremely painful thoughts and memories, they may try to avoid ideas, feelings, conversations, places and, of course, individuals associated with the trauma. In a more or less unconscious effort to avoid such triggers, they will tend to inhibit their emotions. Very often, post-traumatic stress victims experience insomnia, difficulty concentrating, irritability, and a continual fear of being assaulted again. In cases of extreme stress, emotional or cognitive dissociation may take place. Such victims may feel detached, no longer themselves, or not fully conscious; they may experience memory lapses, particularly surrounding the traumatic events themselves.

A girl traumatized by her involvement in prostitution is likely to sustain significant emotional and relational damage. Few adults, even the hardiest ones, would emerge without scars from what most adolescent prostitutes go through, particularly submissives and sex slaves. Many have been victims of gang rape. They have been constantly threatened and physically abused by their pimps and clients. They have witnessed intense violence between gang members and against the girls under gang control. They have seen other youths, both boys and girls, savagely beaten. All the while, they were emotionally isolated and without moral support. In some cases they were physically isolated and reduced to the status of merchandise.

One would assume that the courts, knowing these facts, would show more empathy toward the victims of juvenile prostitution, but many social workers and police officers have the opposite impression. In fact, many judges refuse to acknowledge the girls' status as trauma survivors. Instead of considering them as victims (on a par with incest or sexual abuse victims), they force them to testify as witnesses. It is difficult for anyone to talk about degrading sexual experiences in public, let alone under the cold glare of a prosecutor, but a post-traumatic stress victim is an especially poor witness. Survival, in her case, meant forgetting the causes of her suffering (not to mention that few people in this situation keep a diary!). Under cross-examination, she may experience memory blanks in connection with essential aspects of her testimony. The ordeal may provoke psychosomatic disorders such as insomnia, indigestion, hyperventilation, headaches, trembling, and panic attacks. In fact, the court experience itself may feel like an assault if it brings up stressful memories. The girl's responses may then be perceived by the court as evidence of bad faith or lack of credibility.

A vicious cycle ensues in which the downplaying of victimization leads to aggressive questioning and discrediting of the victims, thus worsening their trauma and increasing the severity of their victimization. This does not serve the interests of the victim or of justice. Therefore, every effort should be made to build the case without resort to the victim's testimony. If it is essential to the case, then the girl must be well prepared and supervised during this demanding process. Numerous practitioners emphasized to us the importance of role-playing, constant reassurance, and psychological support before, during, and after the testimony. Otherwise, the victim is likely to break down, playing into the defendant's hand.

It is worth noting that not all victims display the righteous anger of the stereotypical victim. Girls who have actively participated in their own victimization, particularly the ones we have called the daredevils, or even the submissives, may identify, takes sides with, or even come to the defence of their aggressor. They may oppose his being brought to justice. This dynamic, reminiscent of the "Stockholm syndrome"[28] displayed by former hostages, is often found in cases of physical or sexual assault where the abuser is a trusted person. The fear of injury or death, coupled with the captor's incongruous reassurances, produces a survival reflex in the victim consisting of a cognitive shift. The aggressor comes to seem like a defender. She thinks: "If I identify with his cause, he will hurt me less."

More or less consciously, this reaction is often found in victims of juvenile prostitution, one likely reason why they may be reticent to testify against pimps and clients. Moreover, the secrecy and silence integral to any prostitution ring has become second nature to them. A further complication arises from the manner in which the girls were recruited: not by violent hostage takers but by sweet-talking "lovers." The result is that few girls see their pimps for what they are. They see them as friends, managers, or boyfriends, people with whom they have been sincerely in love. The concept of a pimp never crosses their minds. Meanwhile, the threats, the physical isolation, the wilful erosion of their self-esteem, and the control of their access to other people have increased the pimp's power over them. They cling to the pimp as an object of both fear and love. He may even be perceived as a source of stability in the midst of her distress. We were told that some girls have visited, or attempted to visit, the pimp whom their testimony put behind bars.

Nevertheless, many girls are indeed angry, not just about what they have gone through but also about what the legal system expects of them and about the way it punishes the perpetrators. It is hard enough to testify in public, in the presence of the defendants; if the latter are let off with a slap on the wrist, it only adds insult to injury. Reacting to the light sentencing (fines or community service) of clients in the context of Operation Scorpion, several victims told us they felt disregarded or betrayed by the justice system. So much was demanded of them and of the loved ones, social workers, and police officers who supported them, and all for so little. They were left with a bitter sensation of impotence and injustice.

11

What After-Effects Do Prostituted Girls Experience?

Apart from post-traumatic stress syndrome and Stockholm syndrome, a great many conditions may affect girls who have gone through juvenile prostitution. The typology presented above (sex slaves, submissives, daredevils, and independents) suggests that emotions and feelings may differ depending on the persons involved. The nature and extent of these physical, psychological, emotional, and relational after-effects will depend on the girl's personality, the support available to her, her status within the gang and its culture, her family background, her experience in prostitution, the amount of time she devoted to it, her personal worldview, and any violence inflicted on her or other girls. We have observed that former submissives and sex slaves may experience shame, self-deprecation, and distress. They may feel that their love relationship is on the rocks and that they have lost control over their lives. Conversely, daredevils may initially feel affirmed by their participation in prostitution, viewing it as an opportunity to please others while making money. They may feel affirmed by associating with gang members, meeting "important people" among the clients, having nice clothes, attending private parties, or going on outings. All of this may give them a sense of control over their lives. In a word, they may feel like winners. This explains why these young women may willingly devote themselves to recruiting other girls. Who better than a satisfied person to sell others on the benefits of her activities?

All sorts of rationalizations may make their appearance when girls attempt to define the nature of their work. A young woman who perceives herself as an escort may say, "I don't work the streets. I'm not a whore." She may think, "My clients take me on expensive outings. They like being with a pretty girl. Sex is just an extra." A young woman involved in a love relationship with a pimp may think, "If I sleep with johns to help my boyfriend pay his debts, it isn't prostitution. It's just until things get better." Such attitudes are partly due to the trivialization of sexuality among today's youth. For many young women, sex seems the only way to carve out a place alongside men. They cannot see any great difference between giving a blow job at school to be popular with the boys and servicing a client to help out a boyfriend. Both, ultimately, are ways of making friends and solving problems.

The after-effects of prostitution may vary in intensity and severity. Still, far be it from us to suggest that teenage prostitution can be a beneficial experience. Regardless of the level of involvement, the risk of trauma is significant (Government of Canada 1998; Conseil Permanent de la Jeunesse 2004; Dorais 1987; Durocher and Fleury 2002; Fredette and Fleury 2002; Lane 2003; UNICEF 2001). The research of Fournier, Cousineau, and Hamel (2004) and Knox (2004) clearly indicates that sexual and physical abuse, threats, intimidation with weapons, and other kinds of mistreatment are the daily lot of girls exploited by street gangs. Involvement in criminal activities other than prostitution can have physical and mental consequences as well. To all this may be added the impact of stigmatization, rejection, and social isolation due to societal prejudices. Still today, unfortunately, prostitution is blamed on its unwilling victims.

As it is, the girls used by street gangs are doubly victimized: by the men and boys who use them and by female gang members who try to protect their sexual reputations by treating the others as sex objects, "whores." The submissives and sex slaves targeted by this behaviour may be subjected to repeated acts of verbal, physical, and sexual abuse by other girls. Their sexual victimization may continue without respite until their association with the gang finally ceases.

Research suggests that juvenile prostitution increases the risk of HIV and other sexually transmitted infections that can be serious if not detected and treated. Not all clients or pimps agree to wear condoms, especially with a minor. Unwanted pregnancies may occur. Girls who find themselves as young single parents have had to go back to prostitution to support their families.

In addition, acts of sadism on the part of pimps and clients are depressingly frequent. Girls leaving prostitution often require medium-to-long term medical attention. Many drop out of school, thus hampering their chances of finding other employment.

Emotional and sexual desensitization is another frequently reported consequence. Helping professionals told us that many girls who have had hundreds of sexual encounters are today unable to feel pleasure with a consensual partner. While "sexually experienced" in one sense, they have practised denial or simulation of bodily pleasure for so long that it is no longer a small matter for them to reconnect with their senses. Unfortunately, the mind-body dissociation that is often a matter of survival for young prostitutes, as it is for incest victims, may be long lasting. They need a type of sexual and emotional re-education. Compounding the problem, one victim told us, is an understandable unwillingness to trust men in general, not knowing which of them may be a pimp in disguise.

As with victims of sexual abuse, victims of juvenile prostitution often experience confused and contradictory feelings. The body may feel pleasure while the mind feels pain. In fact, the difference between pain and pleasure may have been blurred in young people subjected to acts that disgust or hurt them, yet also provide erotic stimulation. Pain and pleasure may coexist. And if a girl has experienced sexual gratification, she may feel guilty denouncing her clients or pimp. She may be confused as well as to her own status. How can she perceive herself as a victim? What will her testimony be worth in court? It is hard enough for any human being to interpret his or her sexuality; for young people who have felt discordant emotions, it is harder still.

Many of these girls had their very first sexual relations with street gang members and then with clients (giving the lie to the myth of the "easy woman" – and why is there no such thing as an "easy man"?). This makes it even harder for them to distinguish between consenting and forced sexuality. One cannot assume that persons have experienced satisfaction and abandon just because they have felt physical sensations generally associated with pleasure. For clients of prostituted girls (as for sexual abusers), the girl's feigned or real orgasm is perceived as a sign of her voluntary participation or consent. That is not true, as many victims can attest.

In addition to all of this, a girl's ability to trust others is impaired by her passage through the merciless world of juvenile prostitution and the criminalized environment surrounding it. "Once bitten, twice shy," goes the proverb. Social workers and police officers complain of the difficulties they have in reaching these girls. Their trust must be earned. It is a reflex of self-defence: to survive, they have had to quickly learn the necessity of silence, "forgetting," trusting no one. It would be unreasonable to blame them for it.

The point cannot be overstressed: it is critical for judges and prosecutors in particular to be better informed about the possibility of emotional trauma as a result of sexual abuse experienced in juvenile prostitution.

If the existence of post-traumatic stress syndrome and Stockholm syndrome in this context is ignored, it will not only impair the operation of justice but cause further harm to the victims, particularly when they are expected to testify in court as impassive witnesses. It is imperative to acknowledge their fragility and make allowances for it. Otherwise, what do they gain by cooperating with the justice system? They have suffered enough already.

Another conflictive attitude is sometimes encountered in these young women. They have earned lots of money with their bodies. They have been called beautiful and desirable (an ego boost) by the same men who mistreated and abused them (an ego destroyer). They are now conflicted about their beauty; if somebody remarks upon it, they are immediately on their guard. They have learned the hard way that beauty can be exploited and defiled. They know to look for the hidden agenda under the smiling compliment.

It is not a simple matter for them to return to their original home lives after their experience in prostitution. True, they were under the gang's control, but some of them, the daredevils and independents especially, experienced a freedom and autonomy not easily found elsewhere. As paradoxical as it may seem, some girls equate leaving prostitution with losing their freedom. Identification with the gang, love for the pimp, or Stockholm syndrome may reinforce this impression. The result may be repeated instances of running away until the age of majority is reached or a particularly dramatic event causes the girl to question what she sees as her life choice.

12

How Can These Girls Be Helped?

For a researcher (one of the co-authors) who worked for many years as a caseworker before teaching in this field, it would be unthinkable to write a book on juvenile prostitution without a few remarks about how these young people can be helped.

Has the situation changed at all since the publication of *Les enfants de la prostitution* (Dorais 1987)? At the time, because they were associated with delinquency, juvenile and even child prostitution were perceived as the problem – in fact, the responsibility – of their victims. If the book has accomplished anything, we hope that it has rectified this misconception. Gratifyingly, this tendency to blame the victim has gradually disappeared. Not many experts today will still, as was common then, claim that juvenile prostitution is a problem caused by child perverts! A different conceptual framework has emerged. In this section, we reiterate the premises of the new approach to youth caught up in prostitution. We then specifically apply this approach to street-gang controlled prostitution.

It is important to understand that young people who go into prostitution have needs to be satisfied. As we have seen, there are girls who do so out of attachment or dependence on their boyfriends, and others who believe they can make easy money or lead the exciting life of the movie star. Even girls who wind up as sex slaves initially chose the path of prostitution believing what they were told even when they were being wilfully misled. In many cases, prostitution was seen by the girls themselves (or at least by their boyfriends) as a solution. They were attracted with promises of pleasant things – love, money, adventure – and then cheated.

It cannot be overstressed that for these young people prostitution is a way of meeting certain needs. It is a strategic behaviour essentially geared towards achieving tangible results in the short or medium term. It may be a question of making money, getting by after running away, feeling the camaraderie of the gang or the pimp, or receiving the attention of adult clients. Any one girl may have multiple motivations, as we showed in a previous chapter, although one motivation usually dominates. Ultimately, each person who opts for prostitution has a different set of reasons. It may represent a series of voluntary choices, but more often it represents the absence of choice in the face of life's trials, contingencies, and constraints. Everyone wants to be liked, respected, and acknowledged. Few people would choose to be prostituted by street gangs if given another option!

There is often a great deal of dissonance between the results desired by the girls when they begin as prostitutes and the results actually attained. The gap between reality and expectations may widen to the point that it cannot be ignored, leading the girl to abandon the business. In the absence of dissatisfaction, frustration, or disappointment with the results of prostitution, a girl will probably not want out, nor will she be receptive to outside help. Any attempt to provide it at this stage is doomed to failure.

This understanding of prostitution as a strategic choice must guide our search for alternate strategies. The same needs must be met even as the frustrations and harms caused by pimps, clients, drugs, and so forth are diminished. It is no good resorting to force, threats, or coercion, as street gangs do. These tactics will define us as the enemy, rather than persuading young people to quit prostitution for good. Instead, we must help them to overcome their victimization. Trials of pimps and clients are an important venue for this process, one in which the victims can confront the people who did them harm. Of course, it takes a great deal of courage to stand up to one's abusers in public, but if the victims are supported throughout the process by practitioners, prosecutors, and judges, they can make great strides toward a healthful balance in their lives.

What can we do as practitioners to be attentive to the needs and frustrations of these youths? How can we elicit or support their motivation to leave prostitution or the lifestyle that encourages it? Without offering any magical formulas, here are some principles of intervention that have proven fruitful in practice:

1. Cultivate trust and authenticity in your relations with these young women. Make it clear that you are not there to lecture or blame them. You are not going to lock them up behind bars.[29] Your goal is to understand them, to take a genuine interest in their situation. To do that, you must put yourself in their shoes. But be forewarned: these girls have learned to suss out a person in a matter of seconds. You will not put one over on them, and it may take time to gain their trust.
2. Be willing to learn from these young people, their difference, and their experience of prostitution. This is indispensable to any helping relationship. If you judge them as marginal, deviant, or immature, you will close off an opportunity for dialogue. The more their life experience, characteristics, values, and perceptions differ from yours, the more you can learn from their life history. Open your mind to their modes of expression. Be attentive to their needs and emotions, and be respectful of their differences.
3. Offer alternatives to the disparaging stereotypes with which these young women have been saddled. Agree with them that morality has nothing to do with it. Much of your early work with the girls we have described as submissives or sex slaves will consist of helping them to rebuild a positive self-image.
4. From the first session on, explain to them how you view the phenomenon of prostitution and your own role in helping them get out of it. They may or may not share your analysis, but if the helping process is to

go forward, they need to know where you stand. Hold a frank exchange of views about prostitution, regardless of how similar or different they are. Make it crystal clear that your job is to combat juvenile prostitution, not the girls involved in it.

5 Ask the girl to identify what she sees as the advantages and disadvantages of prostitution. Then ask: Which needs were answered by prostitution? Which needs remain unanswered? Have the girl produce a balance sheet of the positive and negative aspects of her experience. A blank sheet of paper divided into two columns will serve this purpose. She is then in a position to find alternate ways to meet the same needs while also finding solutions to the needs unmet by prostitution.

6 Having identified persistent needs and frustrations, the search for alternate solutions will require a great deal of imagination, innovation, and open-mindedness. These young women are facing the immense task of replacing their whole social network. They will have to jettison gang members, friends, and hangouts. The initial step is to ensure that adequate housing and other services are available. Also needed are more programs and curricula suited to girls who have dropped out of school or fallen significantly behind. Nor should their return to the labour market be taken for granted. Many of the young women we have called daredevils and independents may find their new financial prospects rather unattractive as compared with prostitution.

7 Offer appropriate medical, psychological, and legal assistance as necessary. Health care for untreated sexually transmitted diseases or other health problems must be provided by practitioners sensitive to the phenomenon of youth prostitution. Emotional after-effects such as intrusive thoughts, nightmares, depression, or even suicidality are not rare and obviously require rapid, sustained, expert intervention. Likewise, many of these girls have had their legal rights infringed, while some have infringed the rights of others by participating in crime. All are entitled to enlightened counsel.
8 Many of these girls may be dealing with unacknowledged alcohol or drug addictions, and rehabilitation may be necessary. Assess the situation realistically by asking the girl how much she consumes every day or every week. Do not ask her if she is a drug addict. The same person who has just finished assuring you she has no addiction problem may go on to mention that she spends hundreds of dollars or more per week. Understand, of course, that the road ahead is not an easy one. A psychological – not to mention physical – detox requires motivation and determination, which can be elicited and supported but not coerced. Unfortunately, it may take a physical or psychological breakdown for some girls to recognize their addiction.
9 It is essential for the person to experience some success outside of prostitution as soon as possible. She must be shown tangible proof that her life can change, but such change does not take place in

therapy rooms: it occurs in real and everyday life. As a precondition, the cycle of dependency on the pimp absolutely must be broken, a difficult challenge with girls whose self-image, to say nothing of their image of love, is structured by a desire to please others at all costs. The girl may feel that without another person to depend on she is nothing. In lieu of learning how to love themselves, too many young women prefer to avoid abandonment even at the cost of undergoing humiliation, coercion, and violence on the part of the men who supposedly love them. Ultimately, getting out of prostitution may be as lengthy a process as getting into it.

10. Even girls with intact families will need new bonds of understanding, support, and affection from professionals, parents, other family members, friends, and volunteers. Without them, the girls' attempts to get out of prostitution are likely to fail. Support groups, on the model of groups for victims of sexual assault, can be helpful as well. If trauma was suffered, appropriate professional help is imperative. Finally, the parents will also need support to help them better understand their child. Accepting her as a person does not require them to accept what she has done.

In short, the intervention essentially consists of helping these young women to rebuild and reconceive their lives. Before considering therapies or lockdowns, it is wise to consider something much more basic: a stable life within a safe adult environment. This may well be something they have never known. Have we thought to offer it? Have we helped them identify viable projects and stimulating challenges, the kinds of things that make life such an exciting adventure? Have we helped them focus on gaining control of their lives and realizing their dreams? Working in the shadow of the past, we must help them seize the present moment.

13

How Can Girls Be Prevented from Getting into Prostitution?

The foregoing discussion has made clear that for most of the girls entrapped by street gangs, their entry into prostitution is a gradual process. The earlier and more preventive the intervention in that process, the better. We are, of course, the first to recognize that prevention should focus not only on the girls but also on the clients, who create the demand for juvenile prostitution, and the pimps, who profit handsomely from it. We discuss prevention for gang-prone boys in chapter 14.

To a compassionate observer, the striking, perhaps even mystifying feature of many of these girls' stories is the lack of power they seem to have over their love relationships. Surely they must see other life options than to sacrifice themselves body and soul for the love of a boy! Have they never heard of feminism? Or, to turn the phenomenon around: Has *anyone* ever heard of a young man being prostituted against his will for the love of a woman? To ask the question is to answer it, yet the fact remains that the large majority of the girls we interviewed came to the gangs and to prostitution in search, of all things, of love and affirmation.

What they got was a crude simulacrum of these, but then again, their image of love may have been skewed to start with. The accounts we heard betray an apparently widespread belief that being loved is synonymous with being sexually desired: "If he wants my body, he loves me." Responses such as this reinforce one's impression that today's girls have been sexually educated at the expense of what might be called "love education." So have the boys, for that matter, but they are somehow able to distinguish between sexual attraction and love, while the message apparently absorbed by many girls is that it is perfectly appropriate to confuse the two. If this is not bad enough, prostitution brings a third emotion – contempt – into the equation. Too many clients have learned to act out sexual fantasies involving the verbal and physical degradation of girls, and most of the others are at the very least wilfully blind to the sufferings of the young women whose services they use. "Pretty Woman" Julia Roberts may meet her handsome, charming, caring, ultra-rich Richard Gere in the movies, but most of the stories we heard were far from romantic comedy.

Another factor making girls vulnerable to gangs' advances is the hypersexualization of youth and our society in general. Earlier we discussed the notion of pedomorphism. This cult is bolstered, of course, by the profusion of advertising images that we see every day. One pernicious result is that girls gradually internalize society's objectification of their bodies; they come to identify with the image that others – most critically, men – project upon them. Another is that young people have sex at an increasingly early age, when they are not necessarily ready to cope with the feelings that sex arouses, much less the difficult situations it may create.

We can regret the existence of hypersexualization. We must not, however, use it as a pretext for trivializing juvenile prostitution and the violence that goes along with it. Simply put, blaming the victim is the height of injustice, as society and the courts have already recognized in the case of rape and sexual assault. A girl may be considered pretty or sexy, but that in no way justifies her being treated as an object. Nor is there any reason for young women to have to hide their bodies because some men are supposedly incapable of controlling themselves. The "male urge" – men as slaves to their desires – is largely a myth. It bears frequent repeating that while all human beings feel sexual and other desires, every responsible citizen must learn to accept that these must remain unfulfilled if they infringe the rights of others. Life in society demands no less. The inability to postpone gratification can easily put a man on the road to delinquency and violence.

Only after their escape were the girls able to recognize that emotional dependency and lack of self-confidence had made them naïve and vulnerable to the pimps' seductions. It did not hurt, of course, that the gang members had money, good looks, and buff bodies. Still, that in itself would not have been enough to lure many girls in. The extra element was a distorted image of love that the girls cherished and protected ("I was in love with love," said one), closing their eyes to bad omens such as verbal and physical violence, the pimp's obsession with secrecy, and the spending of large amounts of money that no one seemed to have earned.

The foregoing analysis makes clear the importance of educating girls about love, gangs, and the predictable traps that a person may fall into. In the experience of our respondents, prevention messages are not getting across to members of their peer group as loudly and clearly as they should. A colossal amount of work remains to be done on producing and honing these messages, gathering information on gang-controlled prostitution, identifying rings that exploit minors, and helping girls get out, initially by simply offering them an attentive ear. All of this will require a collective effort bringing together parents and loved ones, social and community workers, the schools, and the police. As long as street gangs and the mafias supporting them (and to a lesser extent the clients) are better organized than the forces combating them, they will have the upper hand. Only a significant mobilization can make meaningful change.

Any educational materials developed and distributed must frontally challenge various stereotypes about the world of prostitution. If girls continue to think that the greatest danger to them is the stereotypical elderly flasher in a public park, for example, they may overlook the more likely sexual predator: the good-looking, well-dressed young man driving an expensive car. Likewise, the girls we have termed daredevils and independents may not readily identify with the image of the passive victim found in certain brochures and theatre pieces currently in circulation. Where the submissive is misled by seduction, the daredevil is attracted by curiosity or a search for strong sensations, and the dissuasive arguments used in her case must differ accordingly. The daredevil may flatter herself that she is stronger than the gang, stronger than the system she wants to explore and exploit: "I thought I was better and smarter than the others. I figured I'd keep my eyes wide open so I didn't wind up anyone's slave. It took me longer to fall, but I ended up just like the others."

Another angle that stands to be further developed is that of civic vigilance. The Quebec Youth Protection Act requires a person who has knowledge of threats to the health or safety of a person under eighteen, e.g., a girl involved in a gang-controlled prostitution ring, to report the case to the authorities, but this provision is rarely enforced. It is essential, according to several of the practitioners interviewed, to make this obligation to report effective. Otherwise, there is a risk that the prostitution of girls will become normalized, allowing the clients and pimps to go about their affairs with impunity while the girls feel subtly blamed for their situation. The goal – to fight prostitution, not prostituted girls – must be kept front and centre.

A constantly recurring suggestion in our interviews was to provide better support to the parents of girls and boys caught up with street gangs. Relatives of the girls rescued by Operation Scorpion complained that the support they were given was too little and too late. It is true that many of them were so bowled over by events that they did not request help. Nevertheless, what help was provided came from community groups and social services which, while not lacking in good will, did not possess the necessary expertise. Where intervention was successful, it was usually due to the proficiency and personal commitment of an individual police officer or social worker.

The importance of family ties in helping girls leave prostitution must be stressed. If a girl is able to put out a distress call or accept help, it is usually because she still has some ties of loving contact with a parent or other family member. She has a much better chance of escaping if she can count on compassionate but critical family support. The absence of family ties may cause a girl to fall back under the domination of the gang.

For parents, however, the acknowledgment or discovery that their child is involved in prostitution can be profoundly upsetting. It may give rise to a whole range of emotions: guilt, anger, sadness, fear, anxiety, impotence, or sense of failure. Parents in this situation may be so traumatized that they gravitate to the extreme of becoming either highly controlling or despondent and fatalistic. In the latter case, they may tend to leave their daughter to her own devices, or place her in the custody of social service institutions until she reaches the age of majority. Clearly, parents may need support to get through this crisis. It is also essential to promote their contact with the child if that contact has become strained or broken (which is often the case). The parent may not understand or accept the child's choices, but must continue to show love and concern for her nonetheless.

Equally problematic is the situation of parents of pimps, who may find themselves coping with difficult feelings in the wake of their son's conviction. Their parenting skills may have met with harsh censure from elements in the community. They may face accusations that they closed their eyes to their son's activities or profited from them in some way. If they are members of visible minorities, their ordeal may be compounded by racism and xenophobia.

Practitioners who work with teenagers are yet another group in need of education and awareness-raising. Several of those we interviewed regretted their insufficient knowledge of street gangs and how they operate. This is understandable, since gang-controlled juvenile prostitution is a relatively new and rapidly evolving phenomenon in this country. Nevertheless, too many professionals today still base their work on preconceived notions and hearsay rather than on valid information, and their prevention efforts suffer as a result. They need information and training with which to confront the new facts on the ground.

Much of the foregoing discussion has concerned itself with primary prevention, intended to minimize girls' incentives to join the gang – in a word, to nip gangs in the bud. This, however, must be complemented with measures to help girls leave prostitution and to keep them from going back, which are termed secondary and tertiary prevention, respectively. Escaping from street gangs is not just difficult: in many cases it is a strenuous feat. Distraught, subject to threats if they implicate others, perhaps poorly understood and poorly supported by their family or community, many girls will remain vulnerable for a long time to come. Intimidation, addiction, and emotional dependency are always available as techniques to bring them back into the fold. Lacking better prospects, they may return to the gang or get caught up in another organization. "Even after you get out, you can easily fall back in. I've known a few who did," said one young woman, conscious of her vulnerability and isolation after leaving the pimp. "He and the gang pursued me for a long time. They made harassing phone calls. They shadowed me. They threatened me and my family and my friends. It really stresses you out." To combat these tendencies, front-line assistance must be offered as part of a concerted intervention protocol for girls under the influence of street gangs. Such a protocol would specify the collaborative roles of the different practitioners and family members. It would describe the kinds of help that girls need and how to react to attempts to intimidate or "retrieve" them. Needless to say, such programs must be adequately funded if they are to work.

14

What about Prevention for Gang-Prone Boys?

As we have stated, our purpose here is not to analyze the phenomenon of street gangs. Still, their key role in juvenile prostitution calls for stepped-up prevention and intervention for boys. If these efforts are to succeed, however, we must comprehend that membership in a gang may meet legitimate needs. Low-income, excluded, or marginalized young males in particular may look to gangs for self-defence and peer-group identification. Why do street gangs appear to meet these needs? Indeed, why do gangs represent such an apparently ideal solution for so many youths? What specific alternatives can we offer them?

If there is one thing we have tried to show with our strategic analysis of motivations, it is that the phenomenon of street gangs is multifarious and complex, and even more so where prostitution is concerned. We have tried to highlight the diversity of motivations for certain individuals to become involved in gangs on a long-term, occasional, or accidental basis. As Hill et al. (1999)

note, the risk factors leading boys to join gangs vary depending on personality, family background, school situation, and peer group and community circumstances. The intervention techniques will be very different for a highly criminalized, hard-core member, say, than for a peripheral supporter or "hanger-on." According to the caseworkers and educators we interviewed, a one-size-fits-all approach will not do; only an approach adapted to the motivations of each boy is likely to succeed. To personalize the approach, one must consider the boy's level of involvement, his desire to leave the gang, the perceived advantages and disadvantages of membership, and the family and social networks available to him. Quite apart from their specific problems linked to street gang membership, many of these boys have had social, school, and family-related difficulties. They may be suffering the after-effects of family negligence, violence, or sexual abuse. They may be addicted to alcohol or drugs and live with low self-esteem. They will need support in their search for new solutions to past or current problems. The road ahead is likely to be discouragingly rough, even more so if the boy's motivation to leave the gang is not very high. It often takes a dramatic event to cause him to question his membership.

As is the case for girls, successful intervention in the case of boys tempted by gang membership demands cooperation among teachers, parents, friends, social workers, community workers, police, and others with whom they come in contact (Spergel 1995, 2007; Howell 1998). According to Klein (1995), failures of prevention are mainly due to a lack of cohesion among these actors. In the United States, Spergel (1995, 2007, and Spergel et al. 2003) created an integrated intervention model in which existing strategies – social intervention, community-leadership mobilization, neighbourhood-citizen participation, creation of alternative job opportunities, and law enforcement – are combined in a coordinated fashion. The effectiveness of such an approach depends on the development of a network for ongoing discussion of information and practices so as to ensure the compatibility and complementarity of the messages conveyed (for example, in terms of the values promoted).

For the purposes of intervention planning, one must distinguish primary prevention from secondary and tertiary prevention. *Primary prevention* essentially seeks to minimize or reduce incentives for young people to join gangs. It attacks the phenomenon at the root by educating them about the phenomenon at a time when the option of joining a gang is merely one among many in their minds. *Secondary prevention* concerns itself with boys who are already involved with street gangs to differing degrees, the goal being to help them to get out. *Tertiary prevention* consists of a range of strategies and techniques for helping boys who have left a gang to find other life alternatives so that they are not tempted to go back.

When considering primary prevention strategies for boys, it is important to remember that street gang members and aspirants share (or have the impression of sharing) the same problems of social adaptation. More often than not, they fundamentally endorse societal norms of success but believe, rightly or wrongly, that they have not been given equal opportunities to succeed – at least, no legal opportunities, which is why they turn towards illegal ones. They perceive the gang as a remedy for felt injustice and a way to acquire enviable social status and income. Almost all the practitioners among our respondents stressed the desperate need felt by these youths to experience personal (and group) success.

Primary prevention should therefore emphasize rewarding, affirming activities for youth, whether at recreation centres or in the schools. They must be encouraged to develop exciting, achievable projects that turn their scholastic, artistic, and athletic talents to profit. What is more, certain studies have found that young people are more inclined to take a positive view of school and work when the aspects of creativity and play are given pride of place. As well, these are good opportunities for practitioners to build trusting relationships with them.

The idea is that through these activities, they will discover or develop their assets and talents. To make their way through the world of street gangs, boys need intelligence, resourcefulness, and know-how. These same qualities can be used in a socially conscious, constructive way if they are channelled into legitimate aspirations – after all, everyone wants and deserves a decent living. An example of such a project is Ottawa's Project Early Intervention, which ran from 1999 to 2003. It offered a life skills development program, a homework club, sports and recreation opportunities, and ongoing support. One important goal of the project was to increase the participants' resiliency to risk factors linked to criminal behaviour. Another promising initiative is Project Adrenaline, developed by three Montreal organizations (Carrefour Jeunesse Hochelaga-Maisonneuve, Maison des Jeunes Kekpart de Longueuil, and Table de Concertation Jeunesse de Bordeaux-Cartierville). It offers gang-prone youths an opportunity to help organize and plan sports, artistic, cultural, and social activities in their neighbourhood. By adding vocational and skills development activities, this project provides a continuum of intervention approaches including prevention, awareness-raising, mobilization, accompaniment, monitoring, reintegration, encouragement, and deterrence as necessary (Quebec 2003).

School can and must play a primary role with boys who feel excluded from academic life (Wood, Furlong, et al. 1997). Spergel (1995) noted that most street gang members have experienced problems of adaptation in school, maintaining that it is imperative to offer them alternative settings such as cooperative learning programs. The idea is to encourage youth to develop solidarity and create new feelings of allegiance. The city of Laval, Quebec, for example, offers a program called "Joining a Gang" that educates fifth and sixth graders about the problems of street gangs, encouraging discussion on the subject (Quebec 2003). Spergel also argues for curricula involving a mix of academic and vocational learning that looks ahead to opportunities for employment and remuneration in the short term. The message to the boys is that they possess all the aptitudes necessary to enjoy a successful career.

Once a boy has joined a gang and had a taste of "easy money," winning him away becomes a much more complicated endeavour. We are fooling ourselves if we think that he will consider a "joe job" a reasonable alternative to his highly lucrative activities. The prospect offered must be not only socially rewarding but also financially remunerative. Developing such prospects will take increasingly imaginative initiatives in a labour market that tends to shut this population out, often because of prejudice. Why not encourage the formation of youth cooperatives in neighbourhoods with high unemployment rates? The solidarity and pooling of talents that knit gangs together could certainly be turned to profit.

Clearly, there are changes of a societal nature that go far beyond individual intervention; after all, the world of gangs is also a culture, a way of looking at the world and adapting to it. As we have seen, gangs originally answered needs of identification, belonging, and self-defence and probably still do today. Before becoming a problem for the boys involved, their relatives and their community, the gang is a solution. Furthermore, and not too surprisingly, there are positive aspects to all gangs, even those that engage in criminal behaviour. Former members have stated that they developed marketing, negotiation, socialization, and strategic skills, albeit largely for purposes of warfare. They learned how to survive under difficult circumstances. To ignore the positive aspects of what they learned is to trivialize skills that may be useful to them if otherwise channelled. These young people cannot rewrite their life history, but they can build upon it.

To do so, they will have to modify their perceptions about society and its injustices. Gangs recruit by playing upon feelings of exclusion and frustration. It is essential to offer alternative community role models with whom aspiring gang members can identify. These may in some cases become mentors who can help them take a different path. The involvement of former gang members in this role would be helpful, if not indispensable. The Quebec media carried a story about a former street gang leader who has become a pastor and a pillar of his community. Former gang members could be recruited as community workers in the schools. This initiative would work on primary and tertiary levels at once. Boys are more likely to trust community workers with whom they identify, while the former gang members will gain the social rewards and income necessary for them to turn their backs on the gangs.

Another factor that should not be overlooked in primary (and even secondary) prevention is the need to alter boys' image of the police and their work. As front-line professionals, the police must try to gain the trust of adolescents and young adults who feel threatened simultaneously by other gangs and the authorities. This distrust encourages many of them to seek protection by joining gangs rather than requesting help from the police. As we have seen, gangs initially arise from a fear of victimization before they become instruments of aggression. The image of the repressive police officer can be demystified, for instance, through active involvement of the police in school programs and other youth activities. But while occasional information sessions on the dangers of gangs do help to raise awareness in the short term, these are no match for the allure of the gang and the peer pressure to join it. Our police respondents suggested that there should be opportunities for social (including athletic) activities that bring together police officers, educators, social workers, and youth from "hot" neighbourhoods so that antagonism may be lessened through alternate forms of interaction.

Concerning secondary prevention, practitioners must keep in mind the many factors militating against success. For one, members of street gangs inevitably make enemies. Inter-gang rivalry is integral to the phenomenon. There is no official ceremony to indicate that a boy has left his gang, and so this new status may not be obvious to other gang members, the police, or social workers. If he meets with repression and coercion at this critical time, the approach may backfire, sending him back to his empathetic buddies. This example shows how important it is for the various practitioners not to be working at cross purposes. The chances of success increase if the initial positive contact has been made before the temptations of gangs become overwhelming. Hawkins, Catalano, and Associates (1992) emphasize the importance of strategies seeking to introduce or amplify protection factors that reinforce a boy's ability to solve his own problems. As suggested by Hébert, Hamel, and Savoie (1997), a prevention strategy will be more effective if it is designed to decrease risk factors, such that a person's weaknesses and the hazards in his environment are counterbalanced by his skills or proficiencies.

A second difficulty in leaving a gang has to do with the boy's level of involvement in it. His buddies may suspect him of wanting to finger them or switch sides. He may face threats or intimidation. At this point, support from the community, especially from former gang members and others, will help to counterbalance these internal pressures. The hard-core member will also be leaving behind friends, social status, protection and probably a source of income (from taxing, drug dealing, fraud, etc.). The process of leaving the gang will take a great deal of individual commitment as well as outside support. No intervention strategy, however well-designed, has much chance of success if the gang member himself does not want to change. This difficulty is, of course, integral to every helping relationship; still, it should be kept in mind, if only to avoid falling into the cynical attitude that little or nothing can be done to help these youths. Anyone, no matter what he is involved in, needs time in which to assimilate changes in his life. Obviously, certain situations may require more urgent action, such as when a youth is threatened by his peers or by rival gang members. In that case, he must be given immediate protection from others (and perhaps himself as well). He may need to be isolated from them until a concerted intervention strategy involving the school, the family, and the community can be devised.

As to tertiary prevention, it is largely a function of revitalizing neighbourhoods through the implementation of activities that allow young people to come into their own (preparation for employment, interaction with other youths, recreation). Preventive strategies that minimize the importance of these structural factors on youth life choices are doomed to failure in the medium and long term. Gangs are only a symptom of social problems; they cannot be eliminated or minimized without society-wide action. Caseworkers in north-end Montreal, a neighborhood hard hit by street gangs, stressed that intervention must focus on both the youths and their environment. Involvement of community members, supported by community resources such as police, social workers, schools, churches, and former gang members, is necessary.

A word or two must be said about the use of law enforcement in cases of gang-controlled prostitution and other instances of urgent necessity. To begin with, the meaning of enforcement needs to be specified, since the form it takes will vary depending upon the underlying objective. Cauchie and Kaminski (2007), basing their work on Pirès (1998, 2006a, 2006b), note that the objectives guiding criminal law enforcement fluctuate between retribution (redressing the harm caused), deterrence (preventing recidivism), rehabilitation (providing moral, psychological, and medical treatment for the offender), and neutralization of the offender (custodial sentencing). In our view, police action should only strive for neutralization if there is an imminent threat of harm (as in juvenile prostitution). However, far from rejecting all forms of punitive intervention, we recognize that it may be necessary as a step towards holding individuals responsible for their acts, particularly where they have committed violence against another person. Neutralization is a means and not an end.

Police and other gang observers have noted an increase in the violence of inter-gang conflict. Gone is the time when street gangs could be considered harmless, "just groups of kids" that would eventually fall apart by themselves. No longer just kids, many of today's gang members are criminalized to an extent that they rival organized crime. Law enforcement has its place: of that there can be no doubt. But it must be used in a way that does not reinforce gang members' feelings of injustice and rejection. Rather, the point is to make them aware of the consequences of their criminal activities. It is a sobering fact that policing has not made much of a dent in the North American street gang phenomenon (Howell 2000; Delaney 2006). A founder of one of the early American street gangs, now on death row, has devoted his life to warning youth of the false solution that gangs represent. Evidently, even the hardest-core gang members can come to their senses – and it should not take a death sentence to make that happen.

The recommendations we have presented ensue from our strategic analysis of street gangs. We could not conclude a work on juvenile prostitution, however, without addressing the issue of male-female relations as perceived by gang-prone youth. This brings us back to the second approach outlined in our introduction, that of gender analysis. We surmise that the socialization of these young men to love and sexuality is partially at fault. Many of them lack positive role models for relations with women. Such models can and should be sought in the family, the church, and the schools. We do not deny that certain cultures, religions, and families inculcate an unequal vision of male-female relations in which men always have the upper hand, but this is all the more reason to seize every public opportunity to present and promote egalitarianism as a model for love and sex.

Schools and youth organizations must provide education about the oppression that is often found in relations between the sexes. Most cultures, it is clear, have traditionally refused to view women as subjects of desire, only as its objects. Similarly in gangs, male desire rules while female desire is denied or manipulated. As long as the wider society tolerates the perception or treatment of women as inferiors, objects, or toys, pimps will feel free to do likewise and point the finger elsewhere. Yet more egalitarian models are achievable. To realize them, love and sex education will be necessary, at school and elsewhere. Consideration should be given as well to the sex role images disseminated via television, music, videos, radio, the Internet, and other mass media. It is important for gang members and other young men to learn that there are other ways to affirm their intersecting identities (gender, sex, group, social, ethnic) than by oppressing women or more vulnerable individuals.

Traditional societies placed tremendous stress on rites of passage, and street gangs have followed in this tradition. Surely it would be possible to develop new rites that mark the recognition of the individual by his community. Only when he feels that he has a rightful place in the community will a boy realize that he does not need a gang in order to establish his identity and personhood. Anything that counters the exclusion and marginalization of youth is a useful component of effective prevention strategies.

Conclusion

The phenomenon of street gangs in our large cities appears, unfortunately, to be on the rise, and prostitution is one of their principal activities. For boys from disadvantaged backgrounds, it is a tremendous ego booster, not to mention a source of profit, to have pretty girls at their beck and call. Indeed, for a great many men this has always been the ultimate sign of social success.

Gangs did not invent juvenile prostitution, but they did redefine it and bring younger girls into the business. Our knowledge of these clandestine phenomena is still woefully inadequate and must evolve in step with changes on the ground. In our survey, some of the answers that we found led to new questions. It became clear that further research must be done on the following critical aspects of juvenile prostitution and gang-linked crime:

- The specific motivations and profiles of boys who become pimps in street gangs. What are their personal and family backgrounds? What percentage of them were themselves victims of physical or sexual abuse? How many have been prostitutes?

- The motivations of the clients of juvenile prostitution, a vastly underexplored area (understandably, as there are obvious methodological and ethical problems with such research).
- The preventive support that is needed to help gang-prone girls and boys avoid the temptations of street gangs, including support to the families and communities.
- The specific factors making girls prone to the seductions of pimps.
- The process of escaping juvenile prostitution, by studying the trajectories of girls who have successfully done so.
- The links between street gangs and other criminal organizations, such as biker gangs and mafias, in connection with the prostitution of girls and young women and with the sex trade in general (including juvenile pornography).
- The involvement of gangs and organized crime in male juvenile prostitution, an emerging phenomenon according to certain respondents.

Both the pimps and the prostitutes who work for street gangs have one thing in common: they do not want to be left behind. They do not want to be losers. Despite or because of their personal, family, or social problems, they do not hesitate to consider any means, licit or illicit, of achieving their goals. It is even possible that some of these boys and the girls who work as their recruiters prostitute girls so that they do not (or no longer) have to do it themselves.

Gang members are, for the most part, "nice boys" who end up doing bad things (viewed from a societal standpoint). As we have said, gangs emerge out of fear and exclusion and only later do they become their agents. How can this vicious cycle be broken? How can the illicit activities of street gangs, pimping in particular, be made less attractive to gang-prone youths? These questions are central to the daily concerns of the practitioners who deal with the problem.

Any discussion of juvenile prostitution remains incomplete without addressing the demand for the service. When clients look at this market in human beings, all they see is its benefits to them in terms of their own sexual satisfaction. Yet desire of any sort is not an incurable malady. We are all responsible for respecting the liberty and bodily integrity of others, and that goes double where the "others" in question are vulnerable minors. As has been done with some success for sexual abusers of children, imaginative publicity campaigns must be developed to confront clients with the clear message that their actions are responsible for hurting minors.

Ultimately, all the parties involved in street gang-controlled juvenile prostitution have strategic interests at stake. The pimps are in it for the money and the status. The clients are in it to break taboos, to preserve the illusion of their youth, or to dominate and degrade others.

And the girls are in it for love, adventure, independence, and earnings. Viewed in terms of these goals alone, it is obviously the girls who are getting the worst of the deal. But viewed from the broader standpoint of loving human relations, it is fair to say that every single party to the transaction is a loser.

Appendices

Appendix One

JUVENILE PROSTITUTION, THE CRIMINAL CODE, AND THE JUSTICE SYSTEM IN CANADA

Some confusion surrounds the role of law enforcement in relation to juvenile prostitution and the protection that it affords girls under the control of pimps. This confusion is partially due to the fact that adult prostitution is not illegal in Canada, although three classes of related activities are illegal:

1 keeping or inhabiting a "common bawdy-house" (section 210 of the Criminal Code of Canada);
2 procuring or living on the avails of prostitution (section 212);
3 communication in a public place for the purpose of engaging in prostitution (section 213).

Unlike adult prostitution, juvenile prostitution is specifically prohibited by the Criminal Code. Section 212 (4) provides:

> Every person who, in any place, obtains for consideration, or communicates with anyone for the purpose of obtaining for consideration, the sexual services of a person who is under the age of eighteen years is guilty of an indictable offence and liable to imprisonment for a term not exceeding five years and to a minimum punishment of imprisonment for a term of six months.

The same applies to procurers of persons under the age of eighteen, an act punishable since 2005 by a minimum prison sentence of two years and a maximum sentence of 14 years. The Criminal Code prohibits living "wholly or in part on the avails of prostitution of another person under the age of eighteen years." Section 212 (2.1) prescribes a minimum prison sentence of five years for procurement of a person under the age of eighteen if:

(a) for the purposes of profit, he aids, abets, counsels, or compels the person under that age to engage in or carry on prostitution with any person or generally, and
(b) he uses, threatens to use, or attempts to use violence, intimidation or coercion in relation to the person under that age.

It is important to remember that minimum sentencing is an exceptional measure in Canada, reserved for crimes considered extremely serious, such as those committed with a weapon or against children.[30] Those who fear that legalization or decriminalization of adult prostitution – as in the Netherlands and New Zealand, respectively – would diminish the legal arsenal available to deal with juvenile prostitution are confusing two different sets of realities and laws. As for those who believe that increasing the age of consent would help to protect prostituted girls, they are forgetting that the age of consent to prostitution is already eighteen. The competent authorities have a range of tools at their disposal with which to protect girls from the violence of prostitution, pimps, and clients, including the assault and sexual assault provisions of sections 265–269 and 271–273.[31] Section 265 is a particularly useful tool against pimps. It stipulates that anyone who, without the consent of another person, applies force intentionally to that other person, directly or indirectly, or attempts or threatens, by an act or a gesture, to apply force to another person is guilty of assault. Section 265(2) clarifies that "assault," for these purposes, includes "all forms of assault, including sexual assault, sexual assault with a weapon, threats to a third party or causing bodily harm and aggravated sexual assault." The maximum prison term for assault is five years (section 266). But there is still a problem with enforcement. While section 265(3) provides that no consent can be presumed where there is application of force, threats or fear of the application of force, fraud, or the exercise of authority, it is up to the judge to decide whether the consent defence is valid or not. But as our study has shown, there is an ambiguous relationship between the prostituted girl and the pimp, who may also be girlfriend and boyfriend. Quite apart from any direct threats made by the gang to her and her family, it is simply difficult for her to testify against the boy she has loved. For this reason, we have recommended that judges be better educated about the social realities of street gangs and the types of prostitution they control, not to mention the distress and ambivalence experienced by the victims.

It should also be recalled that sections 150–153 of the Criminal Code protect children from sexual interference, touching, and exploitation. In light of these sections of the Criminal Code, we see the existing legal framework as sufficient to deal with the sexual exploitation of youth in general, and with juvenile prostitution in particular. The necessary improvements are of a different order: society's minimization or even denial of these realities must be addressed; the legal system must become much more accommodating to the victims; and, in particular, judges must be educated as to the seriousness of the offence of procuring prostituted girls and its after-effects.

Appendix Two

STUDY METHODOLOGY

The research leading to the publication of this book took place over a three-year period. Our study is in fact a combination of three small research projects carried out from 2004 to mid-2006, followed by a fourth in the winter of 2007 to revise and augment the original French text for English publication. As we initially projected, the majority of our respondents, who numbered about fifty, were social workers, community and street workers, educators, and police officers, most of them working in Quebec City and Montreal, with a few in the Gatineau/Ottawa area or in more rural areas. They were interviewed individually or in small groups. It was from them that we first heard numerous accounts of teenage girls prostituted by street gangs (some respondents, especially educators and police officers, have knowledge of a large number of such cases). Subsequently, further to our public comments in the wake of

Operation Scorpion as well as the publication of the French version of this book, we were contacted directly by a few of these young women and by others who have been in similar situations. We interviewed them under strict conditions of anonymity either in person, by telephone, by written account, or by e-mail. A dozen more detailed and extensive personal histories were collected in this way. Unexpectedly, we were also contacted by two parents, one mother and one father (of different girls), who wanted tell their stories. A boy who had worked in gang-related prostitution also contacted us by e-mail, providing details that authenticated his account. We made no attempt to meet with clients.

Our qualitative data collection and analysis obeyed a heuristic approach of sorts. After a first round of interviews and a sufficient review of the literature, we formulated some hypotheses and asked new respondents to critique, contradict, or validate them; then we repeated the cycle. In our view, this ongoing interplay between researchers and field workers was the biggest factor in the success of our study.

Notes

1 In Quebec City in 2002, an investigation dubbed "Operation Scorpion" caused a public uproar when it led to the arrests of several high-profile residents, including a popular radio host. Seventeen girls were rescued from pimps and most of them placed in protective custody.

2 For work from Quebec, see Mathews (1993); Blondin (1993); Hébert, Hamel, and Savoie (1997); Hamel et al. (1998); Lanctôt and LeBlanc (1996, 1997); Grégoire (2001); Tichit (2003); Perreault and Bibeau (2003); and Fournier, Cousineau, and Hamel (2004). We also read certain journalistic accounts where they provided new and relevant data about the phenomenon, particularly expert testimony.

3 See Alex Alonso's well-documented "Black Street Gangs in Los Angeles: A History," on line at http://www.streetgangs.com/history/histo1.html, excerpted from his forthcoming book (based on his

thesis), *Territoriality among African American Street Gangs in Los Angeles.*

4 This term, according to one street worker, can be understood not just in physical but also in metaphorical terms, as an area of competency – for example, drug dealing or prostitution.

5 See, for example, Covey, Menard, and Franzese (1992); Howell (1994); Parks (1995); Spergel (1995); Ball and Curry (1995); Decker and Van Winkle (1996); Shelden, Tracy, and Brown (1997).

6 See Symons (1999) and Grégoire (1998).

7 Certain boys who become pimps have worked in prostitution (heterosexual or homosexual) themselves or were sexually assaulted as children, a subject requiring further research.

8 Very few Canadian studies have been done on girls' involvement in street gangs. Apart from the work of Lanctôt and LeBlanc (1997), which sought to ascertain the level of social and personal adaptation of girl gang members tried in Montreal youth court, and the master's thesis by Céline Grégoire (2001) on the experience of girls affiliated with gangs, all the available research comes from the United States. See, in particular, Burris-Kitchen (1997); Campbell (1990); Chesney-Lind (1989, 1993); Chesney-Lind and Hagedorn (1999); Chesney-Lind and Sheldon (2004); Chesney-Lind et al. (1990); Curry (1998); Esbensen et al. (1999); Knox (2004); Miller (2001); Molidor (1996); Moore and Hagedorn (2001); Peterson et al. (2001); Schalet et al. (2003); Shelden et al. (1996); and Taylor (1993).

9 See, for example, Esbensen and Huizinga (1993) or Esbensen and Winfree (1998).

10 See Campbell (1984a, 1984b); Joe and Chesney-Lind (1995); Esbensen et al. (1999); Deschenes and Esbensen (1999); Fagan (1990); Moore (1991); Molidor (1996); Curry (1998); and Moore and Hagedorn 2001.

11 The event may resemble what some French authors call a *tournante*, although the role of this practice is mainly to punish and humiliate a girl who is considered too independent. It is not necessarily, as in the case of a gang bang, to condition a girl for what awaits her in prostitution.

12 Here we follow the typology of Miller 1975.

13 In the province of Quebec the comic strip "Le silence de Cendrillon" (Cinderella's silence), created and distributed by the Centre Jeunesse de Montréal (Montreal Youth Centre), has done much to alert girls to gangs' tactics.

14 Tutty and Nixon (2003) make the same observation.

15 See Canada, Committee on Sexual Offences against Children and Youths (1984); Canada, Parliament, Special Committee on Pornography and Prostitution (1985); Lowman (1987); Shaver (1996); Canada, Federal/Provincial/Territorial Working Group on Prostitution (1998); and Schissel and Fedec (1999).

16 Tutty and Nixon (2003); Tyler, Hoyt, Whitbeck, and Cauce (2001).

17 Tutty and Nixon (2003) support this hypothesis with the observation that two-thirds of the prostituted

girls they interviewed in the Canadian Prairie Provinces were at some point in their lives in contact with the Child Welfare System.

18 See Joe and Chesney-Lind (1995); Molidor (1996); Miller (1998, 2001); Moore and Hagedorn (2001); Nixon et al. (2002); Fournier, Cousineau, and Hamel (2004). Studies of adult female prostitutes are more divided on this question, some finding these women to be no different from the norm, others finding a pattern of prior victimization; see Geadah (2003).

19 Various studies have underscored the importance of economic aspects in juvenile prostitution. Lane (2003), for example, found that girls' participation was often partially or totally a matter of economic necessity for her or her relatives.

20 We do not address the issue of male prostitution in this book, mainly because it is less under the control of street gangs. See Dorais (2003, 2005), a study dealing specifically with young male prostitution.

21 We distinguish pornography from eroticism on the basis of its manifestly dehumanizing, violent, or even sadistic nature. Pornography eroticizes domination, degradation of others as sex objects, and violence against them. It goes far beyond the mere representation of nudity or consensual, egalitarian relationships of the kind generally seen in erotic art.

22 See www.unesco.org/courier/1999_09/fr/connex/txt1.htm, Guttman (1999).

23 The best known of these is Landslide, located in Fort Worth, Texas, a portal allowing paying subscribers access to child pornography on sites located in Indonesia and Russia; see Rettinger (2000) and Howitt (1995).

24 Three researchers independently evaluated contentious photos and reached the conclusion, with strong inter-observer agreement, that few of the individuals depicted resembled children or teens. The majority of them appeared to be eighteen or over.

25 See, in particular, Conseil du Statut de la Femme (2002); Durocher and Fleury (2002); Fredette and Fleury (2003); Shaver (2005); UNICEF (2001).

26 For a summary of Canadian research on clients, see Lowman and Atchison (2006). Other useful works include Atchison et al. (1998); Lowman (1989); Cooke (1984); and Gemme et al. (1984). For the United States, see Monto and McRee (2005); Monto (2000, 2004); Busch et al. (2002); Sycamore (2000); Prasad (1999); Elias et al. (1998).

27 See Canada, Parliament, House of Commons, Standing Committee on Justice and Human Rights, Subcommittee on Solicitation Laws (2006).

28 Named for a 1973 hostage-taking in that city. For more about post-traumatic stress syndrome and Stockholm syndrome, see Damiani (1997).

29 We concede that it is sometimes necessary to protect a young woman by keeping her out of the world of prostitution and street gangs. However, such a

protective measure should never be conceived of as punishment. Too many victims have been treated in such a way that this essential nuance was lost on them. Besides, there are other ways to protect someone without resorting to placement in a home or, worse, taking away her freedom, at least if she has committed no crime and has displayed any level of motivation to quit the lifestyle.

30 At the adjournment of the 38th Canadian Parliament in 2005, the Criminal Code comprised 42 offences with corresponding minimum sentencing provisions.

31 Section 272(2)(a) on sexual assault with a firearm carries a minimum sentence of four years in prison.

Bibliography

Asbury, Herbert. 1928. *The Gangs of New York: An Informal History of the Underworld*. New York: Knopf.

Astwood Strategy Corporation. 2003. *Results of the 2002 Canadian Police Survey on Youth Gangs*. Ottawa: Department of Public Safety and Emergency Preparedness.

Atchison, C., L. Fraser, and J. Lowman. 1998. "Men Who Buy Sex: Preliminary Findings on an Exploratory Study." In *Prostitution: On Whores, Hustlers and Johns*, edited by J. Elias, V. Bullough, and G. Brewer, 172–203. Amherst, N.Y.: Prometheus Books.

Ball, R.A., and G.D. Curry. 1995. "The Logic of Definition in Criminology: Purposes and Methods for Defining 'Gangs.'" *Criminology* 33, no. 2: 225–45.

Baraby, Jean. 2005. "Les gangs de rue: Une action concertée pour un phénomène complexe et préoccupant." *10 ans de savoir*. Online at www.fcsq.qc.ca/Publications/Savoir/Mars2005/Savoir-Pages-8-9.pdf.

Belitz, J., and D.M. Valdez. 1997. "A Sociocultural Context for Understanding Gang Involvement among Mexican-American Male Youth." In *Psychological Interventions and Research with Latino Populations*, edited by J.G. Garcia and M.C. Zea, 56–72. Boston: Allyn and Bacon.

Blondin, Pierre. 1993. "Les gangs de rue." In *Violence et déviance à Montreal*, edited by Maurice Chalom and John Kousik, 91–103. Montreal: Liber.

– 1995. Les gangs de rue. *Pensons famille* 6, no. 42. Online at www.familis.org/riopfq/publication/pensons42/gang.rue.html.

Bouamama, Saïd. 2004. *L'homme en question: Le processus du devenir-client de la prostitution*. Clichy: Mouvement du Nid.

Burris-Kitchen, Deborah. 1997. *Female Gang Participation*. New York: Edwin Mellen Press.

Busch, Noel Bridget, Holly Bell, Norma Hotaling, and Martin A. Monto. 2002. "Male Customers of Prostituted Women: Exploring the Perceptions of Entitlement to Power and Control and Implications for Violent Behavior toward Women." *Violence against Women* 8, no. 9: 1093–112.

Campbell, Anne. 1984a. "Girls' Talk: The Social Representation of Aggression by Female Gang Members." *Criminal Justice and Behaviour* 11, no. 2: 139–56.

– 1984b. *The Girls in the Gang: A Report from New York City*. New York: Basil Blackwell.

– 1990. "Female Participation in Gangs." In *Gangs in America*, edited by Ronald C. Huff, 168–81. Newbury Park, Calif.: Sage.

Canada. Committee on Sexual Offences against Children and Youths. 1984. *Sexual Offences against Children: A Report of the Committee on Sexual Offences against Children and Youths, Appointed by the Minister of Justice and Attorney General of Canada, the Minister of National Health and Welfare.* Ottawa: Supply and Services Canada.

– Parliament. Special Committee on Pornography and Prostitution. 1985. *Pornography and Prostitution in Canada.* Ottawa: Supply and Services Canada.

– Department of Justice. Federal/Provincial/Territorial Working Group on Prostitution. 1998. *Report and Recommendations in Respect of Legislation, Policy and Practices Concerning Prostitution-Related Activities.* Online at www.justice.gc.ca/en/news/nr/1998/exec.html.

– Parliament. House of Commons. Standing Committee on Justice and Human Rights. Subcommittee on Solicitation Laws. 2006. *The Challenge of Change: A Study of Canada's Criminal Prostitution Laws.* Ottawa: House of Commons.

Cauchie, Jean-François, and Dan Kaminski. 2007. "Éléments pour une sociologie du changement pénal en Occident: Éclairage des concepts de *rationalité pénale moderne* et d'*innovation pénale*." *Champ pénal/Penal Field* 4. Online at www.ppenal.revues.org/document613.html. Viewed 11 February 2007.

Chesney-Lind, Meda. 1989. "Girls' Crime and Woman's Place: Toward a Feminist Model of Female Delinquency." *Crime and Delinquency* 35, no. 1: 5–29.

– 1993. "Girls, Gangs, and Violence: Reinventing the Liberated Female Crook." *Humanity and Society* 17: 321–44.

Chesney-Lind, Meda, and John M. Hagedorn, eds. 1999. *Female Gangs in America: Essays on Girls, Gangs, and Gender.* Chicago: Lake View Press.

Chesney-Lind, Meda, and Randall G. Shelden. c2004. *Girls, Delinquency, and Juvenile Justice.* Belmont, Calif.: Wadsworth/Thomson Learning.

Chesney-Lind, Meda, Randall G. Shelden, and Karen A. Joe. 1990. "Girls, Delinquency, and Gang Membership." In *Gangs in America*, edited by Ronald C. Huff, 185–203. Newbury Park, Calif.: Sage.

Cloward, Richard A., and Lloyd E. Ohlin. 1960. *Delinquency and Opportunity: A Theory of Delinquent Gangs*. New York: Wiley.

Cohen, Albert K. 1955. *Delinquent Boys: The Culture of the Gang*. New York: Free Press.

Conseil du Statut de la Femme. 2002. *La prostitution: Profession ou exploitation? Une réflexion à poursuivre*. Quebec: Conseil du statut de la femme.

Conseil Permanent de la Jeunesse. 2004. *Vu de la rue. Les jeunes adultes prostitué(e)s*. Québec: Conseil Permanent de la Jeunesse.

Cooke, N. 1984. "Working Paper on Pornography and Prostitution: A Report on Prostitution in the Atlantic Provinces." Ottawa: Department of Justice.

Corriveau, Patrice, and Francis Fortin. Forthcoming. *La pornographie juvenile sur Internet: Portrait d'un univers complexe* (working title). Montreal: VLB Éditeur.

Côté, Michelle. 2004. *Portrait de l'exploitation sexuelle des enfants à des fins commerciales. L'initiative du service de police de la ville de Montréal.* Montreal: Service de Police de la Ville de Montréal.

Cousineau, Marie-Marthe. 2004. "Gangs: Un tour du Québec pour faire le pont ... Un forum pour en parler!" *Continuum JC* (Centre Jeunesse de Montréal) 3, no. 1: 3.

Covey, Herbert C., Scott W. Menard, and Robert J. Franzese. 1992. *Juvenile Gangs.* Springfield, Ill.: Charles C. Thomas.

Criminal Intelligence Service Canada. 2003 and 2006. *Annual Report on Organized Crime in Canada.* Ottawa: Criminal Intelligence Service Canada.

Curry, David G. 1998. "Female Gang Involvement." *Journal of Research in Crime and Delinquency* 35, no. 1: 100–18.

Cusson, Maurice. 2005. *La délinquance, une vie choisie.* Montreal, Hurtubise HMH.

Damiani, Carole. 1997. *Les victimes.* Paris: Bayard.

Decker, S.H., and B. Van Winkle. 1996. *Life in the Gang: Family, Friends and Violence.* New York: Cambridge University Press.

Delaney, Tim. 2006. *American Street Gangs.* Upper Saddle River, N.J.: Pearson Prentice Hall.

Deschenes, Elizabeth Piper, and Finn-Aage Esbensen. 1999. "Violence and Gangs: Gender Differences in

Perceptions and Behavior." *Journal of Quantitative Criminology* 15, no. 1: 63–96.

Dorais, Michel. 2003. *Travailleurs du sexe*. Montreal: VLB Éditeur.

– 2005. *Rent Boys: The World of Male Sex Workers*. Montreal: McGill-Queen's University Press.

Dorais, Michel, and Denis Ménard. 1987. *Les enfants de la prostitution*. Montreal: VLB Éditeur.

Dufour, Rose. 2005. *Je vous salue …* Sainte-Foy, Quebec: Éditions MultiMondes.

Durocher, Lise, and Évelyne Fleury. 2002. "La prostitution juvénile, quoi de neuf?" *Défi jeunesse* 9 (November) 1: 23–30.

Elias, James, Vernon Bullough, and G. Brewer, eds. 1998. *Prostitution: On Whores, Hustlers and Johns*. Amherst, N.Y.: Prometheus Books.

Esbensen, Finn-Aage, and David Huizinga. 1993. "Gangs, Drugs, and Delinquency in a Survey of Urban Youth." *Criminology* 31, no. 4: 565–87.

Esbensen, Finn-Aage, and Thomas L. Jr. Winfree. 1998. "Race and Gender Differences between Gang and Nongang Youths: Results from a Multisite Survey." *Justice Quarterly* 15, no. 3: 506–25.

Esbensen, Finn-Aage, Elizabeth Piper Deschenes, and Thomas L. Jr. Winfree. 1999. "Differences between Gang Girls and Gang Boys: Results from a Multisite Survey." *Youth and Society* 31, no. 1: 27–53.

Fagan, Jeffrey. 1990. "Social Processes of Delinquency and Drug Use among Urban Gangs." In *Gangs in*

America, edited by Ronald C. Huff, 183–219. Newbury Park, Calif.: Sage.

Farley, Melissa, Isin Baral, Merab Kiremire, and Ufuk Sezgin. 1998. "Prostitution in Five Countries: Violence and Post-Traumatic Stress Disorder." *Feminism and Psychology* 8, no. 4: 405–26.

Fleury, Évelyne, and Chantal Fredette. 2002. *Le silence de Cendrillon: Prostitution juvénile par les gangs. Guide d'animation et d'accompagnement de la bande dessinée.* Montreal: Centre jeunesse de Montréal – Institut universitaire, Agence de développement de réseaux locaux de services de santé et de services sociaux.

Fournier, Michèle, Marie-Marthe Cousineau, and Sylvie Hamel. 2004. "La victimisation: Un aspect marquant de l'expérience des jeunes filles dans les gangs." *Criminologie* 37, no. 1: 149–66.

Fredette, Chantal, and Évelyne Fleury. 2003. "Membres de gangs cherchent jeunes filles pour exercer le plus vieux métier du monde." *Continuum* JC 2 (July 28) 19: 3–4.

Geadah, Yolande, 2003. *La prostitution, un métier comme un autre?* Montreal: VLB.

Gemme, R., A. Murphy, A. Bourque, M.A. Nemeh, and N. Payment. 1984. *A Report on Prostitution in Quebec.* Working paper no. 11. Ottawa: Department of Justice.

Grégoire, Céline. 1998. "Les gangs de rue: Mythe ou réalité?" *Défi jeunesse* 5, no. 1: 18–22.

– 2001. "Lorsque les jeunes filles affiliées aux gangs racontent leur expérience: Ce qu'elles en disent." Master's thesis, Université de Montréal.

Guay, J.P. 2007. *Vers un modèle circomplexe des gangs de rue*. Montreal: Forum d'orientation de recherche FQRSC: Le phénomène des gangs de rue.

Guttman, Cynthia. 1999. "Paedophilia: The Darker Side of the Net." *UNESCO Courier* (September). Online at www.unesco.org/courier/1999_09/uk/connex/intro.htm.

Hagedorn, J.M. 1998. "Gang Violence in the Postindustrial Era." In *Youth Violence*, edited by Michael Tonry and Mark H. Moore, 365–419. Chicago: University of Chicago Press.

Hamel, Sylvie, Chantal Fredette, Marie-France Blais, and Jocelyne Bertot. 1998. *Jeunesse et gangs de rue. Phase II: Résultats de recherche-terrain et proposition d'un plan stratégique quinquennal*. Montreal: Service de police de la Communauté urbaine de Montréal.

Hanson, Kitty. 1964. *Rebels in the Street: The Story of New York's Girl Gangs*. Englewood Cliffs, N.J.: Prentice-Hall.

Hawkins, J.D., R.F. Catalano, et al. 1992. *Communities That Care: Action for Drug Abuse Prevention*. San Francisco: Jossey-Bass Publisher.

Hébert, Jacques, Sylvie Hamel, and Ginette J. Savoie. 1997. *Plan stratégique, "Jeunesse et gangs de rue."* Phase I: Literature review. Montreal: Institut de recherche pour le développement social des jeunes (IRDS).

Hill, K.G., J.C. Howell, J.D. Hawkins, and S.R. Battin-Pearson. 1999. "Childhood Risk Factors for Adolescent Gang Membership: Results from the Seattle Social Development Project." *Journal of Research in Crime and Delinquency* 36, no. 3: 300–22.

Holzman, H. and S. Pines. 1997. "User Buys: Why Men Buy Sex." *Australian and New Zealand Journal of Criminology* 30: 55–71.

Howell, J.C. 1994. "Recent Gang Research: Program and Policy Implications." *Crime and Delinquency* 40, no. 4: 495–515.

– 1998. *Youth Gangs: An Overview.* Washington: Department of Justice, Office of Justice Programs, Office of Juvenile Justice and Delinquency Prevention.

– 2000. *Youth Gang Programs and Strategies.* Washington: Department of Justice, Office of Justice Programs, Office of Juvenile Justice and Delinquency Prevention.

Howitt, D. 1995. *Paedophiles and Sexual Offences against Children.* New York: John Wiley.

Huff, Ronald C., ed. 1990. *Gangs in America.* Newbury Park, Calif.: Sage.

Jankowski, Martín Sánchez. 1994. "Les gangs et la presse: La production d'un mythe national." *Actes de la recherche en sciences sociales* 101–2: 110–17.

Jenkins, P. 2001. *Beyond Tolerance: Child Pornography on the Internet.* New York: New York University Press.

Joe, Karen, and Meda Chesney-Lind. 1995. "Just Every Mother's Angel: An Analysis of Gender and Ethnic Variations in Youth Gang Membership." *Gender and Society* 9, no. 4: 408–31.

Klein, M.W. 1995. *The American Street Gang: Its Nature, Prevalence, and Control.* New York: Oxford University Press.

Knox, George W. 2004. "Females and Gangs: Sexual Violence, Prostitution, and Exploitation." *Journal of Gang Research* 11, no. 3: 1–15.

Lanctôt, Nadine, and Marc LeBlanc. 1996. "La participation des garçons à une bande marginale: Un phénomène de sélection et d'opportunités." *Canadian Journal of Criminology* 38: 375–400.

– 1997. "Les adolescentes membres des bandes marginales: Un potentiel antisocial atténué par la dynamique de la bande?" *Criminologie* 30, no. 1: 111–30.

Lane, Erin C. 2003. "Correlates of Female Juvenile Delinquency." *International Journal of Sociology and Social Policy* 23, no. 11: 1–14.

Legardinier, Claudine, and Saïd Bouamama. 2006. *Les clients de la prostitution.* Paris: Presses de la Renaissance.

Lovell, R., and C.E. Pope. 1993. "Recreational Interventions." In *The Gang Intervention Handbook*, edited by A.P. Goldstein and C.R. Huff, 319–32. Champaign, Ill.: Research Press.

Lowman, John. 1987. "Taking Young Prostitutes Seriously." *Canadian Review of Sociology and Anthropology* 24, no. 1: 99–116.

– 1989. *Street Prostitutes: Assessing the Impact of Law.* Vancouver, Ottawa: Department of Justice.

Lowman, John, and Chris Atchison. 2006. "Men Who Buy Sex: A Survey in the Greater Vancouver Regional District." *Canadian Review of Sociology and Anthropology* 43, no. 3: 281–96.

Lucchini, Riccardo. 1996. "Femme et déviance ou le débat sur la spécificité de la délinquance féminine." Online at www.unifr.ch/socsem/Fichiers%20PDF/Femme%20&%20deviance.pdf.

Mansson, Sven-Axel. 1986. "L'homme dans le commerce du sexe." Study produced for UNESCO. In *La prostitution aujourd'hui, actes de la 3e Université d'automne intitulée "Au marché du sexe, le client, qui es-tu?" Mouvement le Cri*, November 1993.

Mathews, Frederick. 1993. *Youth Gangs on Youth Gangs*. Ottawa: Department of the Sollicitor General, Police Policy and Research Division.

Miller, Jody. 1998. "Gender and Victimisation Risk among Young Woman in Gangs." *Journal of Research in Crime and Deliquency* 35, no. 4: 429–53.

– 2001. *One of the Guys: Girls, Gangs, and Gender.* New York: Oxford University Press.

Miller, Walter B. 1975. *Violence by Youth Gangs and Youth Groups as a Crime Problem in Major American Cities*. Washington: Government Printing Office.

Molidor, Christian E. 1996. "Female Gang Members: A Profile of Aggression and Victimization." *Social Work* 41, no. 3: 254–7.

Monto, Martin A. 2000. "Why Men Seek out Prostitutes." In *Sex for Sale: Prostitution, Pornography and the Sex Industry*, edited by Ronald Weitzer, 67–83. New York: Routledge.

– 2004. "Female Prostitution, Customers and Violence." *Violence against Women* 10, no. 2: 160–88.

Monto, Martin A., and Nick McRee. 2005. "A Comparison of the Male Customers of Female Street

Prostitutes with National Samples of Men." *International Journal of Offender Therapy and Comparative Criminology* 49, no. 5: 505–29.

Moore, Joan W. 1991. *Going Down to the Barrio: Homeboys and Homegirls in Change*. Philadelphia: Temple University Press.

Moore, Joan W., and John M. Hagedorn. 2001. "Female Gangs: A Focus on Research." Online at www.ncjrs.org/html/ojjdp/jjbul2001_3_3/contents.html#acknowledge.

National Youth Gang Center. 2006. *National Youth Gang Survey: 1999–2001*. Washington: Department of Justice, Office of Juvenile Justice and Delinquency Prevention.

Nixon, Kendra, and Leslie Tutty. 2003. "'That Was My Prayer Every Night – Just to Get Home Safe': Violence in the Lives of Girls Exploited through Prostitution." In *Being Heard: The Experiences of Young Women in Prostitution*, edited by Kelly Gorkoff and Jane Runner, 69–85. Black Point, N.S.: Fernwood.

Nixon, Kendra, Leslie Tutty, Pamela Down, Kelly Gorkoff, and Jane Ursel. 2002. "The Everyday Occurrence: Violence in the Lives of Girls Exploited through Prostitution." *Violence against Women* 8, no. 9: 1016–43.

Parent, Colette, and Christine Bruckert. 2005. "Le travail du sexe dans les établissements de services érotiques: Une forme de travail marginalisé." *Déviance et société* 29, no. 1: 33–53.

Parks, C.P. 1995. "Gang Behavior in the Schools: Reality or Myth?" *Educational Psychology Review* 7, no. 1: 41–68.

Perreault, Marc. 2005. "Les gangs de rue: Un passage risqué. Quelques pistes de réflexion pour comprendre la violence dans les milieux marginaux des jeunes Québécois d'origine afro-antillaise." In *Jeunesse à risque: Rite et passage*, edited by Denis Jeffrey, David Le Breton, and Joseph Josy Lévy, 57–68. Sainte-Foy: Presses de l'Université Laval.

Perreault, Marc, and Gilles Bibeau. 2003. *La gang: Une chimère à apprivoiser. Marginalité et transnationalité chez les jeunes Québécois d'origine afro-antillaise.* Montreal: Boréal.

Peterson, Dana, Jody Miller, and Finn-Aage Esbensen. 2001. "The Impact of Sex Composition on Gangs and Gang Member Delinquency." *Criminology* 39: 411–39.

Pirès, Alvaro P. 1998. "Aspects, traces et parcours de la rationalité pénale moderne." In *Histoire des savoirs sur le crime et la peine*, vol. 2, *La rationalité pénale et la naissance de la criminologie*, edited by Christian Debuyst, Françoise Digneffe, Jean-Michel Labadie, and Alvaro Pirès, 3–52. Ottawa: Presses de l'Université d'Ottawa.

– 2006a. "Tomber dans un piège? Responsabilisation et justice des mineurs." In *La responsabilité et la responsabilisation dans la justice pénale*, edited by Françoise Digneffe and Thierry Moreau, 217–46. Bruxelles: Larcier.

– 2006b. "Questions – réponses sur la rationalité pénale moderne." Unpublished working paper, Université d'Ottawa.

Prasad, M. 1999. "The Morality of Market Exchange: Love, Money and Contractual Justice." *Sociological Perspectives* 42, no. 2: 181–214.

Quebec. 2003. *Création d'un réseau québécois d'échanges. Les jeunes et les gangs de rue: Faut plus qu'en parler!* Quebec: Government of Quebec. Online at www.msp.gouv.qc.ca/prevention/prevent/progfina/produits/actes_colloque_fev03.pdf.

Rettinger, L. Jill. 2000. *The Relationship between Child Pornography and the Commission of Sexual Offences against Children: A Review of the Literature.* Ottawa: Department of Justice Canada, Research and Statistics Division.

Rice, R. 1963. "A Report at Large: The Persian Queens." *New Yorker* 39: 153–87.

Schalet, Amy, Geoffrey Hunt, and Karen Joe-Laidler. 2003. "The Articulation and Meaning of Sexuality among the Girls in the Gang." *Journal of Contemporary Ethnography* 32, no. 1: 108–43.

Schissel, B., and K. Fedec. 1999. "The Selling of Innocence: The Gestalt of Danger in the Lives of Youth Prostitutes." *Canadian Journal of Criminology* 41: 33–56.

Shaver, Frances M. 1996. "Prostitution: On the Dark Side of the Industry." In *Post-Critical Criminology,* edited by Thomas O'Reilly-Fleming, 42–55. Scarborough, Ont.: Prentice-Hall Canada.

– 2005. "Sex Work Research: Methodological and Ethical Challenges." *Journal of Interpersonal Violence* 20, no. 10: 1–24.

Shelden, Randall G., Sharon K. Tracy, and William B. Brown. 1996. "Girls and Gangs: A Review of Recent Research." *Juvenile and Family Court Journal* 47, no. 1: 21–39.

– 1997. *Youth Gangs in American Society*. Toronto: Wadsworth/Thomson Learning.

Souillière, N. 1998. *Youths and Gangs: Various Views, Random and Varied Strategies*. Ottawa: Canadian Police College Research Centre.

Spergel, Irving A. 1964. *Slumtown, Racketville, Haulburg*. Chicago: University of Chicago Press.

– 1995. *The Youth Gang Problem: A Community Approach*. New York: Oxford University Press.

– 2007. *Reducing Youth Gang Violence: The Little Village Gang Project in Chicago*. Lanham, M.D.: AltaMira Press.

Spergel, I. A., K.M. Wa, S. Grossman, A. Jacob, S.E. Choi, R.V. Sosa, E.M. Barrios, and A. Spergel. 2003. *The Little Village Gang Reduction Project in Chicago*. Chicago: University of Chicago.

Starbuck, D., J.C. Howell, and D.J. Lindquist. 2001. *Hybrid and Other Modern Gangs*. Office of Juvenile Justice and Delinquency Prevention.

Stinchcomb, Jeanne B. 2002. "Promising (and Not So Promising) Gang Prevention and Intervention Strategies: A Comprehensive Literature Review." *Journal of Gang Research* 10, no. 1: 27–45.

Sycamore, M., ed. 2000. *Tricks or Treats: Sex Workers Write about Their Clients*. New York: Harworth Press.

Symons, Gladys L. 1999. "Racialization of the Street Gang Issue in Montreal: A Police Perspective." *Canadian Ethnic Studies* 31, no. 1: 124–38.

Taylor, Carl S. 1993. *Girls, Gangs, Women and Drugs*. East Lansing: Michigan State University Press.

Thornberry, Terence P., Marvin D. Krohn, Alan J. Lizotte, Carolyn A. Smith, and Kimberly Tobin. 2003. *Gangs and Delinquency in Developmental Perspective*. Cambridge, U.K.: Cambridge University Press.

Thornburg, D., and H.S. Lin. 2002. *Youth, Pornography and the Internet*. Washington: National Academic Press.

Thrasher, Frederic M. 1927. *The Gang: A Study of 1,313 Gangs in Chicago*. Chicago: University of Chicago Press.

Tichit, Laurence. 2003. "Gangs juvéniles et construits ethniques dans le contexte américain." *Criminologie* 36, no. 2: 58–68.

Totten, M.D. 2000. *Guys, Gangs, and Girlfriend Abuse*. Peterborough, Ont.: Broadview Press.

Tutty, Leslie, and Kendra Nixon. 2003. "'Selling Sex? It's Really like Selling Your Soul': Vulnerability to and the Experience of Exploitation through Child Prostitution." In *Being Heard: The Experiences of Young Women in Prostitution*, edited by Kelly Gorkoff and Jane Runner, 29–44. Black Point, N.S.: Fernwood.

Tyler, K.A, D.R. Hoyt, L.B. Whitebeck, and A.M. Cauce. 2001. "The Effects of a High-Risk Environment on the

Sexual Victimization of Homeless and Runaway Youth." *Violence and Victims* 16, no. 4: 441–55.

UNICEF. 2001. *Profiting from Abuse: An Investigation into the Sexual Exploitation of Our Children.* New York: UNICEF, Division of Communication.

Vigil, James Diego. 1990. "Cholos and Gangs: Culture Change and Street Youth in Los Angeles." In *Gangs in America,* edited by Ronald C. Huff, 116–28. Newbury Park, Calif.: Sage.

– 2002. *Rainbow of Gangs: Street Culture in the Mega City.* Texas: University of Texas Press.

Ville de Quebec. 2005. "Rapport du service de police sur les gangs de rue et la prostitution juvénile: La sécurité de nos jeunes: une priorité constante, March 7." Online at www.ville-quebec.qc.ca/fr/information/communique/protection_publique/2562.shtml.

Wood, M., M. Furlong, J. Rosenblatt, L. Robertson, F. Scozzari, and T. Sosna. 1997. "Understanding the Psychological Characteristics of Gang-Involved Youths in a System of Care: Individual, Family, and System Correlates." *Education and Treatment of Children* 20: 281–94.

Index